Healthful & Cuisine

Anna Maria Clement, Ph.D., N.M.D.
with Chef Kelly Serbonich
and Celebrity Chef Chad Sarno

HIPPOCRATES
HEALTH INSTITUTE

A
HIPP◐CRATES
HEALTH INSTITUTE
Publication

Publisher
Brian R. Clement , Ph.D., N.M.D., L.N.

Cover Art and Design
Jim Scattaregia

Food Preparation & Styling
Peter Cervoni

Photography
Kenneth Appelbaum
Michael Steinbacher

Hippocrates Health Institute
1443 Palmdale Court
West Palm Beach, Florida 33411
(561) 471-8876
www.HippocratesInstitute.org

Third Edition, 2013
Second Edition, 2009
First Edition, 2006

Medical Disclaimer: The food, food preparation and health information in this book is based on the training, experience and research of the authors and is intended to inform and educate. Check with a qualified health professional prior to beginning this or any health program. The author and publisher specifically disclaim any liability, loss, or risk, personal or otherwise, which is incurred as a consequence, directly or indirectly, of the use and application of the contents of this book.

ISBN 978-0-9771309-4-8

This publication is printed on recycled paper and made with soy-based inks. Hippocrates replenishes more than the amount of trees required to print this publication, through www.coolingtheplanet.org

Contents

Acknowledgments

I would like to thank each and every person who has worked by my side at the Brandal Clinic in Stockholm, Sweden, and Hippocrates Health Institute in West Palm Beach, Florida. Their efforts and those of the hundreds of thousands of guests who have attended our health programs have enriched both my soul and my education. Special thanks to Chef Kelly Serbonich; without her focused and dedicated help this recipe book would not have come to fruition. I would also like to thank Master Chef Chad Sarno for the special recipes he contributed to enhance this edition. I see a day when the world's people can live harmoniously through becoming personally responsible for all things, including the food they consume.

Anna Maria Gahns Clement
Ph.D., N.M.D., L.N.C.

I would like to thank everyone who has influenced me on my path as a raw food chef. To those chefs I have had the pleasure of working with and learning from, and who have facilitated the development of this book. To David Hirth (who first taught me about raw food preparation), Peter Cervoni and Ken Blue, I am deeply grateful for having had the opportunity to share, grow, and learn with you. To Brian and Anna Maria Clement, you have facilitated the enrichment of my life in countless ways, and I'll never feel that I've thanked you enough. Your generosity and spirit forever influence and motivate me. Finally, to all whom I've had the privilege of teaching and interacting with at Hippocrates and elsewhere, you have been the driving force behind this book—it is for you. Go further and reach even higher in your quest for health, happiness and vitality.

With all my love and blessings,
Kelly Serbonich

Anna Maria Gahns Clement
Ph.D., N.M.D., L.N.C.

Dr. Anna Maria Gahns Clement embarked on her professional career as a practitioner of natural health care when she assumed the directorship of the Brandal Clinic in Stockholm, Sweden, an internationally recognized and well-respected center for health recovery. Her single-minded mastery of skills as a Ph.D. nutritionist, naturopathic medical doctor, iridologist, bodywork therapist, touch-for-health facilitator, nursing health care provider and scientific weight loss expert served to enhance her instinctive healing abilities and qualities.

She founded the first living-food organization in Scandinavia and was a member of the Natural Health Care Coalition, a government-supported effort in unifying the field of complementary health care in her native Sweden.

For more than three decades she has been co-director and chief health administrator of Hippocrates Health Institute, originally located in Boston, Massachusetts and now in West Palm Beach, Florida. Dr. Clement is considered one of the leading experts in intuitive diagnostics, a revolutionary research tool that assesses a person's state of health.

Anna Maria Gahns Clement is the author of several books on the application of natural health methods in family and children's care. She also collaborated in creating a series of books and DVDs about the Hippocrates Life-Transformation Program, and addresses groups globally on the importance of taking responsibility for all aspects of their lives. She embodies a down-to-earth, sensible approach in teaching practical methods that people can comfortably incorporate into their own lives.

As multi-faceted as her life is, Anna Maria considers her role as mother to her four children – and grandmother to their children – as the most important, most challenging and most enjoyable work of all. The exemplary health of the Clement family is a tribute to her and the Hippocrates lifestyle.

About the Authors

Dr. Clement is considered one of the leading experts in health analysis, a revolutionary research tool that assesses a person's state of well-being.

Chef Kelly Serbonich

 Kelly has had a lifelong interest in food and how it affects people. Inspired by her grandmother's love, and by the way in which she brought people together in celebration through food, Kelly's deepest desire was to recreate the closeness and happiness that food and celebrations bring. She began her career in food at the age of 16 by flipping burgers and cooking french fries! After high school she studied culinary arts at Johnson & Wales University (Providence, RI), obtaining an A.A.S in Culinary Arts.

Kelly's personal and professional interest in a vegetarian, and eventually a vegan, lifestyle began after she encountered many unexplainable health issues in college, some leading to hospitalization. Searching for answers, Kelly earned a B.S. in Culinary Nutrition. It was through this program and a graduate internship requirement that she learned about the Hippocrates Health Institute.

At the Hippocrates Health Institute, Kelly embraced the raw-food lifestyle and all of her health challenges soon disappeared. She was and continues to be both fascinated and enthralled by the power of the Hippocrates program. Shortly thereafter, Kelly became Hippocrates' Executive Chef. She embraced the challenge of preparing foods that were not only healing and pure, but also had enough taste appeal to inspire guests to prepare them when they returned home. Little did she know that inspiring the guests would be simple when acting as an example and when being true, real, and down-to-earth about what she most believes in and acts upon.

Kelly believes that her mission is to pour her energy, love and positive attitude into the food, and through this, the process of preparing heavenly and divine foods becomes effortless. Kelly's goal is to prepare food while teaching people ways to foster healing and growth that are practical enough for everyone. Her greatest reward, which is constant and endless, is seeing people transform themselves from dull and dying to alive and radiant. Kelly is the delighted mother of a healthy son, Noah Serbonich, and resides in the Finger Lakes Region of New York State. Prior to Noah's birth, she was a chef at the renowned Moosewood Restaurant in Ithaca, NY.

About the Authors

Kelly's greatest reward, which is constant and endless, is seeing people transform themselves from dull and dying to alive and radiant.

Executive Chef Chad Sarno

Called "The king of uncooked and vegan cuisine, and chef to the stars" by *GQ* magazine, and "the Michael Jordan of living foods" by actor Woody Harrelson, Chad Sarno is one of the world's leading vegan chefs.

Chad has brought his approach to healthy cuisine to some of the world's premier organic vegan restaurants, spa resorts, film sets, healing centers and individual clients for more than two decades.

Chad grew up in restaurants and, as gastronomy is a family passion, with the delicious and comforting home-cooked meals of his mother and paternal Italian grandmother. He was raised with the vibrant flavors of fresh produce from his mother's garden, which made him aware of the 'garden to table' philosophy in which he believes strongly.

When Chad first embraced a living foods diet, he realized that the emphasis in most healthy eating programs is on the physical body. The emotional aspect of eating is ignored, but for many of us, food is not just physically but emotionally fulfilling. This motivated him to experiment with traditional recipes, creating healthy versions of his family and childhood favorites.

Throughout his years of training, V.I.P catering and consulting, many celebrities and musicians have enjoyed Chad's culinary services and innovative dishes: Coretta Scott King, Woody Harrelson, Lauren Bacall, Red Hot Chili Peppers, Charlize Theron, Sissy Spacek, Frances McDormand, Niki Caro, Helen Hunt, Tommy Hilfiger, Heather Mills-McCartney, Donna Karen, Jane Fonda, Bobby Weir, Mickey Hart, Bruce Hornsby, George Clinton and many more.

Chad partnered with the LifeCo in mid-2006 to help people realize that moving toward a more plant-based diet can be fun and full of flavor as well as being healthy. He developed the Saf (Turkish for "pure") Cuisine vegetarian restaurant concept in Istanbul, Turkey. Chad also consults with Whole Foods Market and travels worldwide, making appearances and speaking at select health conferences.

 This symbol indicates a recipe provided by Guest Chef **Chad Sarno**.

Chad has brought his approach to healthy cuisine to some of the world's premier organic vegan restaurants, spa resorts, film sets, healing centers and individuals for more than a decade.

There is a struggle happening in our world, whether we choose to recognize it or not, between two cultural forces: the *Culture of Death* – the predominant culture in the world today – which is bringing us misery on every level from war and oppression to poverty, global warming and widespread chronic disease, including depression and addiction; and the *Culture of Life* – represented by works such as *Healthful Cuisine* – which brings us health, well-being, and a joyous spirit. With each choice we are indeed either promoting death or life. And where is this Culture of Death more obvious than in our food system?

At a recent point in history, natural, pure foods were deemed inconvenient and impractical for the feeding and care of the masses. The food industry, in search of solutions, turned their attention to economics and preservation and away from nutritional quality, and we are paying the price. Our cultural emphasis on highly processed, dead and denatured foods, including junk foods, foods that contain high levels of toxic chemicals such as antibiotics, hormones, preservatives, and herbicides, and foods that are modified genetically for the purposes of rendering them impermeable to disease and decay, is resulting in unprecedented levels of illness and chronic disease. Astonishingly, the insanity does not end here. We can now add the most diabolical process to this long and ever-expanding litany of food adulterations – cloning. Yes, as we write, digestive systems across the globe are now engaged in the challenge of "assimilating" cloned animals – animals who are wholly created, through

Foreword

the "wonders" of modern science, in a laboratory. Worse yet, if you do consume animal products you have no way of knowing whether you are consuming a cloned animal or one created through natural order, as currently there is no label law requiring this distinction. It is difficult to imagine that in just a short 50 years we have created – and must now face – such deleterious and dangerous scenarios once the exclusive territory of science fiction novels. Makes me wonder if "Mad Cow" disease should be renamed "Mad Human" disease.

Thankfully, there are organizations, like Hippocrates Health Institute, who have a rich and successful history in – and commitment to – reversing the madness. In fact, for over 50 years Hippocrates Health Institute has been at the forefront of educating people about the Culture of Life. They have worked diligently, through educational programs and publications such as *Healthful Cuisine*, to promote a healthy and conscious lifestyle based on raw and living plant foods. They have also successfully taught hundreds of thousands of people how to overcome sickness and disease through positive, life-affirming choices.

To this end, *Healthful Cuisine: Accessing the Lifeforce Within Through Raw and Living Foods* is an exceptional contribution. This creative work by Hippocrates Health Institute's Co-Director Dr. Anna Maria Clement and former Hippocrates Chef Kelly Serbonich, is a bright and vibrant testimony to the power of the *Culture of Life*. It is an excellent book on every level, and a real treasure!

Healthful Cuisine offers us the Culture of Life through diet with its fresh, organic, unprocessed, plant-source only way of eating, presented in these beautifully balanced, easy-to-prepare recipes. Although sophisticated on one level, the recipes are surprisingly straightforward, demonstrating Dr. Clement's and Chef Serbonich's deep understanding of the nutritional and healing properties of raw & living foods, and appreciation for the culinary excellence and taste that can be achieved through simplicity. The addition of recipes from celebrated raw food culinary master and former *Tree of Life* Executive Chef Chad Sarno brings unique flavor and spark to this already high-impact cuisine book.

Prior to recent decades, people didn't have educated choices, but recipe books like *Healthful Cuisine* are making it comfortable for us to choose health. I highly recommend *Healthful Cuisine* to anyone who desires to cultivate their background and skill in preparing live and raw foods, and increase their enjoyment of food and of life itself.

Gabriel Cousens, MD, MD(H)
Diplomate American Board of Holistic Medicine, Diplomate in Ayurveda
Director of the Tree of Life Rejuvenation Center, Patagonia, AZ

Introduction

With the ever-emerging interest in and commitment to raw, living foods diets, Hippocrates Health Institute felt it timely to present a clear and concise recipe book authored by two generations of living foodists. Chef Kelly Serbonich, one of the outstanding experts whom The Institute has had the privilege to nurture, along with my wife, Dr. Anna Maria Gahns Clement – a woman of vast culinary experience – offer recipes that will satisfy even the most discerning palates. In this third edition, we have the great pleasure of introducing gourmet creations from one of the industry's leading chefs – Chad Sarno. Chef Sarno is known world-wide for innovative and delectable foods that inspire a great appreciation for the beauty, flavor and spirit of raw food cuisine.

Food is not only for pleasure; it has the potential to be a powerful aid in reducing disease and prolonging life. Healthful Cuisine unites the finest tastes and textures with the most life-building and health-promoting foods.

With our busy lives, industrial foods and their marketing allies have seduced us into thoughtless preparation and mindless consumption. We are becoming ill and obese as fast food has become a way of life for individuals and families. This is why Anna Maria and Kelly have made sure that these recipes are not only delicious, but easy to prepare. This type of "fast food" is the fast track to a healthier and more vibrant life. We can no longer wait on the sidelines, but must participate in our personal and planetary healing. Your food choices not only determine your future but also that of our planet.

Every morsel of pure food we consume moves us a step closer to physical and mental realization. We must rekindle our true instincts by choosing fresh, organic, unprocessed, plant-based cuisine which will inevitably enrich every aspect of our lives. Eat well and be well!

Brian R. Clement, Ph.D., N.M.D., L.N.C.
Co-Director, Hippocrates Health Institute

"Food is not only for pleasure; it has the potential to be a powerful aid in reducing disease and prolonging life."

Stocking Your
Kitchen

Chapter I

THE WELL-STOCKED KITCHEN makes for convenient and hassle-free food preparation. Take time to experiment with new and unfamiliar ingredients; it is fun to learn about new foods and herbs and they can greatly enhance your culinary experience. If they aren't available at your local farmers' market, co-op or health food store (most are now), try the internet where you will most certainly find everything! Organic and local foods are ideal choices; growing your own is even better. Our resource list on page 141 will help you locate some of the following equipment and ingredients.

JUICER

A juicer that does more than just juicing is ideal, not only because it is more versatile but also because the gears on these juicers turn more slowly, generating less heat and resulting in a fresher and more nutritious product. We recommend a twin-gear or single-auger juicer. With either of these juicers, you can make patés, nut butters, cookie batter and ice cream, as well as juice.

BLENDER

Unlike a juicer, a blender processes at a much higher speed and does not separate the fiber from the juice of the food product. A blender is used to make items such as dressings, soups, sauces, puddings and smoothies. A high quality blender such as the K-Tec Champ HP3 or Vita-Mix will make raw life much easier! You can even grind spices and nuts in such blenders, and any blended mixture will be smoother and more evenly combined.

FOOD PROCESSOR

This piece of equipment is generally used for chopping or for combining thick mixtures such as salsas, spreads and sauces. Some very thick sauces or mixtures, where a chunky consistency is desired, are perfect for a food processor. Many food processors have attachments for slicing and shredding. Most will be adequate for raw food preparation; however, two things to look for and keep in mind are the sharpness of the blade and the capacity of the food processor bowl. We recommend an 11-cup capacity for average household use.

FOOD DEHYDRATOR

A food dehydrator is very helpful in assisting you to remain on raw food. It will add to the enjoyment of your living foods program by adding creative differences in texture, appearance and flavor. A dehydrator simply removes water. The changes you can expect when dehydrating food include shrinkage, concentration of flavor, crunchy or chewy textures, longer shelf life, and darker color. Dehydration can add a "cooked" appeal without actually cooking food. It is important that you remember to dehydrate foods at or below 115 degrees Fahrenheit or 40.5 degrees Celsius. At this temperature the enzymes are not being lost due to heat, so the food is technically still raw.

SPICE GRINDER

A spice grinder (a.k.a. coffee grinder) is useful for grinding whole spices, small quantities of nuts, and flax seeds. You can even grind your own flour from dried sprouted grains or nuts. While either of the strong blenders mentioned will grind, we've found that the spice grinder uses less electricity and generates less heat. Simply use smaller quantities in the spice grinder. This tool can be found at most stores that sell home goods.

SPIRALIZER

If you ever liked pasta and noodles, you will want a spiralizer. Use any root vegetable or squash to turn out pasta in a minute! With certain models, you can also choose different sizes for your noodles and make beautiful ribbons as well. Prices range from $30 – $100.

UTENSILS

Sharp knives with which you are comfortable contribute to a far more enjoyable experience in the kitchen. We prefer ceramic knives because they have cleaner edges, are lighter, cause less oxidation of the food, and have prolonged edge retention. For most people a chef's knife, paring knife and serrated knife (slicer) are adequate.

OTHER RECOMMENDED GADGETS

salad spinner
strainer
colanders
large mixing bowls
funnel
peeler
measuring cups and spoons
large cutting board
spatulas (rubber and offset)
glass jars with lids
garlic press
kitchen shears
sprout bag (a mesh bag that is also called
    a nut-milk bag)
mandolin

Call 561.471.8876 or visit
wwwHippocratesInstitute.org to order
many of these products and more.

Use organic ingredients whenever possible! Organic produce is higher in nutritional content and is generally free from pesticides, herbicides, fungicides and genetically modified organisms (GMOs).

DRIED INGREDIENTS

Grains: millet, quinoa, amaranth, teff, rye, spelt, kamut, wheat, buckwheat (hulled and unhulled) and oat groats

Beans/Peas: mung, garbanzo (chick pea), whole lentils and whole green peas

Other Seeds for Sprouting: fenugreek, alfalfa, clover, radish, broccoli, onion, cabbage, mustard, chia and unhulled sunflower

Nuts/Seeds (all raw): almond, Brazil nut, walnut, sesame, pumpkin, sunflower (hulled), pecan, macadamia, pistachio, hemp and flax

Dried Herbs/Spices: Below are two lists of everything we have in our kitchen. Some of these spices we use very rarely, but we are including them all to give you ideas on various options

The spices we use most frequently: basil, caraway seed, cayenne, celery seed, curry powder, crushed red chili pepper, chili powder, cinnamon, clove, coriander, cumin, dill weed, fennel seed, garlic powder, ginger powder, Italian seasoning, mustard seed, Mexican seasoning, nutmeg, onion flakes, onion powder, oregano, paprika, pizza seasoning, rosemary, sage, tarragon, thyme and turmeric

The spices we use infrequently: allspice, anise seed, star anise, bay leaf, cardamom, Chinese 5-Spice powder, dill seed, garam masala, marjoram, peppermint leaf, poppy seed, vegetarian poultry seasoning, psyllium husks powder and pumpkin pie spice

Salt Substitutes*: Bragg's Liquid Aminos, Nama Shoyu, dulse seaweed, kelp powder and dehydrated celery powder (homemade)

Sea Vegetables: arame, hijiki, nori sheets, whole leaf nori, whole leaf kelp, kelp powder, wakame, sea lettuce, whole leaf dulse, dulse flakes, fuchus, sea palm and sea vegetable salad mix

Organic Produce** (most commonly used): cucumber, celery, fresh sprouts, onion, garlic, red, orange, or yellow bell pepper, cabbage, dark leafy greens, broccoli and/or cauliflower, avocado, zucchini and/or yellow squash, root vegetables and lemon

Organic Fruit *** (if applicable): whatever is fresh, ripe, and in season, as well as dates, dried figs, raisins and dried apricots

---

*   The best salt protocol is to use no added salt, deriving the organic sodium from food itself.

**   This is only a small sample of what you might use or find in the way of organic produce.

*** Hippocrates Health Institute recommends eliminating fruit consumption if you are dealing with a health challenge.

Food-Combining Wisdom

Chapter 2

THE HUMAN PHYSIOLOGY IS AMAZING. It adapts and changes readily as circumstances change. An important piece of information that people often miss is this: Just because we can do something doesn't mean we should. Digestion is just one of the many topics to which this statement applies. While many people can comfortably combine any and every food in a meal, that doesn't necessarily mean that this is the best thing to do. In fact, in most cases it is not. The effects of improper food combining will accumulate over time and can bring about serious disorders later in life.

At Hippocrates we have seen that poor food combining leads to degeneration. What we know is that different enzymes are required to digest different food components, and that these enzymes are active only when conditions, mainly pH, are right. Digestive conditions are ideal only when we eat proper combinations of food. Food combining is based on knowledge of body chemistry. It includes consuming food in such a way as to make the best of our digestive system with the least effort and challenge to the body. The more purely and cleanly that we eat, the more sensitive we become to the effects of poor food combinations.

The adverse reactions many people experience when eating certain foods often stem from how they are combining those foods. Allergies develop when undigested proteins remain in our system. Allergies are a perfect example of what can happen when we don't combine food properly. Got intestinal gas? It may be because you are spreading nut butter all over your grain bread! Combining foods that have different digestive requirements, such as grains and nuts, can cause gas because of fermentation or lack of proper and complete digestion.

Following proper food combining not only makes digestion easier, it boosts the immune system. Did you know that thirty percent or more of our energy is used to digest food? When we combine foods properly we use less energy to digest and have more energy for other activities. Additionally, when the blood is clean, the cells receive more nutrition and oxygen, which in turn creates a healthier, stronger and more disease-resistant body. Try it for yourself—you will feel and enjoy the benefits.

IN TERMS OF FOOD COMBINING
ALTHOUGH NOT ALL-INCLUSIVE, THESE ARE
REPRESENTATIVE LISTS.* **

WHAT IS A VEGETABLE?
All lettuces and greens, celery, cabbage,
cauliflower, broccoli, cucumber, asparagus,
celery root, kohlrabi, yellow summer squash,
zucchini, bell pepper, carrot, sea vegetables, beet,
turnip, parsnip, radish, all herbs, onion, scallion,
garlic, sprouted lentils, sprouted mung beans,
sprouted adzuki beans, sprouted fenugreek,
all small sprouts such as alfalfa, onion, clover,
broccoli and radish. (Avg. 2½ hours digestion
time)

WHAT IS A STARCH?
All sprouted and cooked grains; all hard
winter raw or cooked squash such as butternut,
pumpkin, acorn, etc., sunchokes (Jerusalem
artichokes); all cooked root vegetables (carrot,
beet, rutabaga, turnip, sweet potato, etc.);
sprouted chick peas (garbanzos), sprouted
peas and most sprouted beans. (Avg. 2½ hours
digestion time)

WHAT IS A PROTEIN?
Includes all nuts and seeds such as sunflower,
pumpkin, hemp, sesame, chia, etc.
(Avg. 4 hours digestion time)

WHAT IS A MELON?
These large round fruits come from
plants of the gourd family. They have
edible, fleshy fruit and many seeds.
(Avg. 15-30 minutes digestion time)

WHAT IS A SWEET FRUIT?
Banana, all dried fruit, fresh date and
persimmon. (Avg. 4 hours digestion time)

WHAT IS A SUB-ACID FRUIT?
Fresh fig, pear, peach, apple, grape, mango,
apricot, most berries, plum, cherimoya, cherries,
nectarines, papaya, litchis and tomato.
(Avg. 2 hours digestion time)

WHAT IS AN ACID FRUIT?
Grapefruit, orange, tangerine, sour apple,
pineapple, strawberry, pomegranate, kiwi,
kumquats, loquat, starfruit, cranberry,
loganberry, lime and sour fruit. (Avg. 1 hour
digestion time)

WHAT IS A FAT?
Oils, nuts and avocados.
(Avg. 4 hours digestion time)

* The Hippocrates Store and website carry charts
and books on food combining. Call 561.471.8876
or visit www.HippocratesInstitute.org to order.

** All foods are categorized by their strongest traits,
although they may be composed of several of the
groups listed here.

THE 10 COMMANDMENTS OF
FOOD COMBINING & DINING

1. Consume food and beverage at room temperature—hot and cold temperatures alter enzyme activity and thus affect digestion and tax the body.

2. Avoid drinking 30 minutes before and 2 to 3 hours after eating.

3. Avoid combining protein and starch.

4. Avoid eating more than one type of protein at a time (this does NOT mean you cannot combine more than one variety of nuts or seeds at a meal). The same goes for fat: KEEP IT SIMPLE.

5. Avoid combining more than one fat/protein. For example, don't use avocado, oil and nuts in a dressing; choose just one of these.

6. Eat fruit only with other similar types of fruit. Also, eat fruit only on occasion and when not facing a health challenge. You may combine sweet fruit with sub-acid fruit and sub-acid fruit with acid fruit, but avoid combining acid fruit with sweet fruit.

7. Eat melon alone or only with other types of melon.

8. Avocados go well with either vegetables or fruit, as do onions, garlic, flowers and some herbs.

9. Eat greens and veggies with EITHER avocado OR nuts and seeds OR starchy foods.

10. It is always best to combine as few ingredients as possible for ideal digestion. In the wild, would you expect to find a banana tree next to an apple tree next to an onion plant, or a macadamia nut tree next to a northern pea bush? Wild animals usually eat one food at a time, as did humans for thousands of years before food-processing technologies.

BREATHE…CHEW…SAVOR…AND BE THANKFUL WHEN YOU EAT…
IT WILL HELP YOUR DIGESTION AND YOUR SPIRIT!

Basic Recipes and Procedures

CHAPTER 3

SOAKING & SPROUTING

EASIEST SOAKING

Soaking removes the enzyme inhibitors in nuts, seeds, grains and beans so that they are easier to digest. Soak them overnight or during the day while you are at work. This will ensure 8 – 12 hours of soaking, which covers the entire range of times you will see in sprouting charts from various sources. Soak in pure water at room temperature. Always drain and rinse after soaking and dispose of soaking water.

EASIEST SPROUTING

There are many ways to learn the easy and incredibly rewarding process of sprouting. Hippocrates offers classes, books and a video on growing wheatgrass. Call the Hippocrates store for more information. Other books and videos are available through various internet websites.

HOW TO EAT MORE SPROUTS!

Sprouting is by far the least expensive and easiest way to get incredible nutrition and benefit from Mother Nature's powers. We cannot emphasize enough the importance of sprouts in your diet! If you are seriously having trouble eating your sprouts or just want new ways to enjoy them, we have included some suggestions below. You can use any type of sprout: lentil, sunflower, buckwheat, clover, mung bean, broccoli or any of your liking.

- Make a blended soup and add some sprouts.

- Add them to any salad recipe you like. We mean ANY recipe. If the sprouts are large, chop them up small. You'll never know they are in there!

- Make a green wrap (see Green Wrap basics on page 30) and put lots of sprouts inside.

- Make nori rolls (see Nori Roll basics on page 28).

- Juice and combine them with other juices such as cucumber and/or celery.

- Skip the lettuce and make sprouts the bulk of your salad. Sunflower and pea greens (two powerhouse sprouts) make great bulky salad sprouts.

- Any time you eat dehydrated crackers, eat sprouts with them. Add a little bit of sprouts with every bite of cracker or make mini sandwiches.

AS YOUR HEALTH GROWS, SO WILL YOUR TASTE FOR SPROUTS!
AND AS YOUR CONSUMPTION OF SPROUTS GROW, SO WILL YOUR HEALTH

JUICING & BLENDING

Juicing is the process of separating the liquid (juice) from the fiber of sprouts, fruits and/or vegetables.

Juice is easily digestible and highly nutritious, making it an excellent food source. At Hippocrates we serve juice two times a day. Incorporating a minimum of one organic green juice per day has proven to be extremely beneficial in transitioning to and maintaining a raw and living-foods diet.

Blending is the process of using a blender to combine ingredients to achieve a liquefied, smooth, uniform mixture.

A high-powered blender such as the Vita-Mix or Champ EZ Blend is recommended but not absolutely necessary. Blending breaks food down very quickly and can generate heat, so blend only until you have reached the consistency you desire. Ideally, blended food should be consumed immediately following the blending process because blending reduces the nutrition in the food. However, if this is not possible, do the best you can.

Hippocrates' Green Juice

(Yield: 2 Cups)

1½ cucumbers
3 stalks of celery
4 cups combination of sunflower and
 pea green sprouts

Feed ingredients through a single or double auger juicer. Drink within 20 minutes for optimal nutrition. Other greens that are commonly used to make green juice: kale, Swiss chard, parsley, spinach, lettuce and beet and turnip greens.

BASIC VEGETABLE JUICE

Use the basic Hippocrates' Green Juice and add cabbage, leafy greens sprouts and weeds.

USES FOR BLENDING

• liquefying anything that you would like to be completely pureéd. Very useful for those with chewing or dental challenges, and helpful for those with intestinal problems or severe digestive disorders

• making dressings and sauces, either to sprinkle on or marinate a salad

• making soups—blended soups are fast, easy meals and enable you to get nutrition in an easily digestible form.

• making fruit sauces and creams

• making puddings

DRESSING BASICS

Dressings are an optional way to flavor and tenderize vegetables.

While dressings are not necessary, most people starting out on raw and living food diet use them. Typically, a dressing includes a fat, an acid, salt, sugar, seasonings/flavorings and liquid. It is best to stick with one source of fat when making a dressing so that it is easier to digest. The types of fats to choose from include: avocado, high quality, cold-pressed unrefined oils (such as extra virgin olive, flax, hemp or raw sesame), nuts or seeds. Whole foods such as nuts are always preferred over food isolates such as oils. Seasoning and flavorings can include anything from dried herbs to spices to your choice of fresh herbs and vegetables. From both a flavor and a health perspective, garlic, ginger, turmeric, and cayenne are great additions to any dressing. Liquid is usually needed to blend and adjust the consistency of a dressing. Use pure water or any vegetable juice for this purpose. The use of salt, sugar and acid leads us to our next topic: the four basic tastes. The most popular dressings achieve a balance of the four tastes. Sometimes a fifth one, spicy hot, is included. Here are the ingredients we typically use at Hippocrates to achieve balance in our dressings:

SWEET

stevia (whole leaf, powder or liquid) and naturally sweet vegetables (carrot, red bell pepper, sweet potato). For the sake of optimal digestion and food combining principles, as well as reducing sugar intake, we do not use dried fruit, dates, honey, maple syrup or agave to sweeten food that will be combined with vegetables and other items.

SALTY

dulse (whole leaf, flakes or powder), kelp powder and any other sea vegetables, Bragg Liquid Aminos, Nama Shoyu, ground dehydrated celery, spinach, chard, kale (the green leafy vegetables also add bitterness) and sun-dried olives. Salt generally enhances flavor. When you see the ingredient labeled "flavor enhancer of your choice" in our recipes we are referring you to this section to choose which ingredients, if any, you prefer.

SOUR

fresh lemon juice and raw sauerkraut—you will not find any type of vinegar in our recipes. While raw apple cider vinegar has many beneficial uses, it is less than ideal for mixing with food because it interferes with digestion.

BITTER

dark leafy greens, fresh herbs, unsalted olives and certain oils.

WHAT TO USE WHEN YOU WANT TO THICKEN

zucchini, yellow squash, powdered spices, ground flax seed, psyllium powder, nut/seed butters, soaked nuts/seeds, avocado or oil.

DRESSING BASIC (continued)

Hippocrates' House Dressing

(Yield: 1½ Cups)

1 cup high quality oil
2¼ tablespoons fresh lemon juice
2½ tablespoons Bragg's Liquid Aminos
   or Nama Shoyu

2 cloves garlic
2 teaspoons ground mustard seed
   (or mustard powder)
¼ teaspoon cayenne pepper

Add a few tablespoons of pure water while blending to ensure the emulsion. This dressing can be flavored in hundreds of ways. Add any vegetable to enhance flavor and nutrition, your favorite fresh herbs, or your favorite seasonings, such as Mexican, Indian, Italian, or Cajun. You may also use ginger and change the oil to raw sesame for an Asian-style sesame ginger dressing. This dressing will be referenced throughout the book. It is always ideal to use dressings right after blending them. If your daily schedule does not allow this, do the best you can and use a dressing for a few days. This dressing will last longer than any other type of dressing listed here, at least a week in refrigeration. However, it will not be as vital and nutritious as when first prepared.

Basic Avocado Dressing

(Yield: 1½ cups)

1 avocado
1½ tablespoons fresh lemon juice
1½ tablespoons chopped onion
1 clove garlic

1 cup water or vegetable juice
½ tablespoon Bragg Liquid Aminos
   or Nama Shoyu, optional

Yummy suggestions include adding cucumber, red bell pepper, carrot juice, ginger or lots of fresh herbs. Avocado-based dressings are typically one-day dressings due to the rapid oxidation and breakdown of avocado once its skin is broken.

DRESSING BASICS

Basic Nut/Seed Dressing

1 cup soaked nuts/seeds or nut butter
1-1½ cups pure water or vegetable juice
1 clove garlic   *Add almonds*

1 tablespoon Bragg Liquid Aminos
    or Nama Shoyu, optional

Again, add your favorite fresh herbs and spices. The higher the fat content of the nuts, the shorter the life of the dressing. Nut and seed dressing will usually start to ferment within three days.

Basic Blended Soup

liquid
avocado or nuts/seeds
fresh vegetables
fresh herbs   *Add almonds*

Add liquid to adjust consistency.

Basic Pudding

1 avocado or 1 cup young coconut meat
1 cup dried fruit soaking water, coconut water or pure water
12 dates, pitted & soaked
cinnamon to taste

This is a great pudding base. Add any of your favorite fruits, carob powder, vanilla or other flavorings. Delicious and creamy!

PROCEDURE

1. Roughly chop all ingredients to be blended. The smaller the ingredients are chopped, the easier it will be for the machine to process them. Either mix everything in a bowl and then transfer it to the blender, or just put everything directly into the blender container.

2. Blend until desired consistency is achieved, but for only as long as it is absolutely necessary.

3. Season to taste. Always taste before declaring you are finished! Just because you don't like it immediately doesn't mean you have to throw it away. You can always adjust for taste and blend again to get the mixture to where you want it to be. If you aren't sure what to add to get the flavor you are seeking, refer to the previous information about the four basic tastes. Over time you will see that your taste buds improve and that you know just what to add.

MARINATING BASICS

Marinating is the process of allowing a food to soak in a seasoned liquid typically consisting of an acid, oil, salt and flavorings/seasonings.

Marinating softens food and infuses flavor, creating the sensation of a cooked product.

USES FOR MARINATING

* softening and infusing flavor into vegetables and fruit

* creating salads and other raw dishes

* tenderizing and infusing flavor into sprouted beans, legumes, and grains

Basic Recipes

Savory: For marinating vegetables, tough green leaves and sprouts, use the Hippocrates House Dressing as a base and choose your own flavorings and fresh herbs to modify it.

Sweet: For marinating fruit for desserts, fruit salad or pie fillings, start with 1 cup coconut water blended with vanilla and dates. Add spices such as cinnamon, clove, ginger, cardamom, mint, allspice, etc. accordingly. For a creamier marinade, add ½ cup soaked macadamia or pine nuts, or ¼ -½ cup nut or seed butter.

PROCEDURE

1. **In a bowl:** Place the food to be marinated in a bowl. Pour the marinade over the food and toss to coat. Press the product down in the bowl, so as to submerge it in the liquid as much as possible. Cover and let stand anywhere from 30 minutes to overnight. NOTE: Food will marinate faster at room temperature; however, it is not advisable to leave prepared food at room temperature for more than a few hours.

2. **In a bag:** This method is best when working with very little marinade. Toss the product to be marinated in a bowl with the marinade. Transfer the contents of the bowl into a "biodegradable" plastic bag for food storage. Squeeze out as much of the air as possible and seal or tie off the bag. Let stand anywhere from 30 minutes to overnight.

PATÉ BASICS

A paté is a smooth, rich, typically well-seasoned mixture of vegetables, flavorings, and most commonly, nuts and/or seeds.

Patés are processed using either a food processor, or a twin-gear or single auger juicer, which homogenizes (recommended.) A paté made through a juicer will generally be much smoother and creamier than one made in a food processor. Tip: If using a food processor, add a little nut or seed butter (i.e. sesame tahini, almond butter) to create a smoother and creamier paté.

USES FOR PATÉS

- accompaniment to a salad

- hearty dip for vegetable sticks and chips

- stuffing for vegetables, then dehydrate (optional) vegetable with filling

- filling in nori rolls (see Basics: Nori Rolls page 28)

- filling for raw leaf wraps (see Basics: Green Wraps page 30)

- cracker dough/batter (see Basics: Dehydrating page 40-41)

- burger base (just add chopped veggies, form into patties and dehydrate overnight)

- nut loaf base (just add chopped veggies/herbs, form into a loaf overnight)

Basic Recipe

1 part soaked nuts/seeds
1 part chopped vegetables plus any
   seasonings/flavorings

Note: parts are measured by volume: for example, 1 cup walnuts: 1 cup chopped cauliflower and onions.

The ratio of nuts/seeds to vegetables will vary in recipes; this is just a basic starting point. Generally, the paté will be lighter and more easily digestible when using more vegetables than nuts/seeds.

PROCEDURE

1. Drain soaked nuts/seeds and add to a mixing bowl.

2. Add chopped vegetables and flavorings/seasonings to the bowl. The smaller the vegetables are chopped, the easier it will be for the machine to process them. Toss all together.

3. Using the homogenizing (blank) attachment of an appropriate juicer, or the S-blade of a food processor, process the mixture.

4. Mix well by hand. Taste! Stir in any other desired ingredients (minced onion, celery, fresh herbs, etc.).

Second Option Dehydrated

NORI ROLL BASICS

A nori roll is a cylindrical food product that is made by rolling up ingredients inside a sheet of nori seaweed and sealing it with a small amount of water. Most people recognize nori from Japanese sushi restaurants, where it is most commonly found.

USES FOR NORI ROLLS

- makes an easy meal—also helps get a good variety of vegetables in you, including more sprouts

- party food—slice into 6-8 pieces for a sushi look

- jerky-like snack food—place a thin strip of paté inside and roll up, then dehydrate

Basic Recipe

1 sheet nori
  either:
  ¼ cup nut/seed paté, or
  3 avocado slices, or
  ¼ cup wet, marinated salad
¼ cup shredded vegetable
1 scallion or asparagus spear
2 julienne strips of red bell pepper
½ cup sprouts

Suggestions for other vegetable ingredients are: leafy sprouts, shredded carrot, squash, rutabaga, daikon, black radish, beet, turnip, burdock, sunchoke; horseradish and/or turmeric; any julienne of vegetable. Serve nori rolls with your favorite dip or dressing—wasabi sauce (wasabi powder mixed with water) and/or sesame ginger dipping sauce (sesame oil, garlic, ginger, lemon juice, Nama Shoyu or Bragg Liquid Aminos).

PROCEDURE

1. A bamboo sushi mat is very handy for this task, although not absolutely necessary. Lay the sushi mat on a flat surface. Line the edge of 1 sheet of nori up with the edge of the mat that is closest to you. You will be rolling away from yourself.

2. All ingredients will be placed on the nori in horizontal lines, so that if you were to cut into the completed roll at any two points, you would see the same interior. Start with the moist ingredient first (paté, avocado, or marinated salad) and place a plump line of it across the nori.

3. Next place the other ingredients you wish to include, making a line of each across the sheet of nori.

4. Prepare to roll! Use your fingers to wet the edge farthest from you with pure water. This will seal the roll upon completion of the rolling process. The initial rollover and tuck is the most critical part of the rolling process. Lift the mat along with the nori and other roll contents up and over the piled ingredients and tuck tightly to complete the first rollover.

5. At this point, release the mat, pulling forward and rolling the remainder of the nori. When you lift up the mat, be sure the nori sheet is tucked completely under so that you can finish the rolling process. Voila!

6. Allow the completed roll to sit for 5-10 minutes before cutting. This will soften the nori a bit and make it easier to cut cleanly.

7. Slice and serve!

GREEN WRAP BASICS

A wrap is a combination of food in which there is typically an outside "shell" and a semi-damp inside combination of ingredients. The shell— in this case a green leaf of some kind—acts as a carrier for consuming the inner ingredients, just as bread holds a sandwich together.

USES FOR GREEN WRAPS

- substitute for cooked wraps and a popular easy way to eat a good meal

- kids' lunches

Basic Recipe

**1 large leaf of your choice,
  either:
  ½ cup paté, or
  ½ avocado sliced, or
  ½ cup of your favorite thick dip
¼ cup sauerkraut (optional, but highly
  recommended)
torn dulse leaves
½ cup sprouts
¼ cup shredded veggie sauce or dressing of
your choice, optional**

Ideal leaves for wrapping: collard greens, large romaine leaves, large kale leaves, red leaf lettuce leaves, and any large green leaf. Romaine hearts are great for tacos; collard greens are great for burritos.

PROCEDURE

1. Place your leaf as open as possible on a flat surface.

2. Place your pate, avocado or thick dip in first, making a lengthwise line. Top with any other ingredients you are including. Depending on the leaf, either roll up or just fold and enjoy.

3. Instructions for rolling a collard burrito: Follow the previous instructions for loading up the leaf. Next fold the stem and top edge of the leaf inward.

4. Roll from one side to the other to complete the burrito-like wraps. Slice in half.

5. Enjoy!

COOKIE/PIE CRUST BASICS

A cookie is a dessert varying in shape, size and texture—from bite-size and cake-like, to fist-size, thin and crispy.
Cookies can be small rounds, bars, logs, frosted cutouts, or chewy squares. Raw cookies are sometimes called "rawies" (since no actual cooking takes place.) A raw cookie typically consists of nuts or seeds and dried or sticky sweet fruit. Some cookies also contain sprouted grains.

A pie crust is a shell that contains a filling.
Conventional pie crust is made from flour, butter, salt and water. Raw pie crusts are usually made from chopped or ground nuts or seeds, and a little dried fruit to bind and slightly sweeten.

Any cookie recipes can be made into a pie crust as well.
Just press the cookie mixture into a pie plate. Dehydrating the crust is an ideal step, but not necessary, before adding the pie filling.

WHEN CLOSELY ADHERING TO FOOD COMBINATIONS, YOU MAY ADD STEVIA AND APPLE PECTIN TO THE MIX RATHER THAN FRUIT OR DRIED FRUIT.

USES FOR COOKIES & PIE CRUSTS

- desserts—for special occasions

- holidays

- snacks (especially for kids)

- introducing people to raw foods and healthier desserts

Basic Recipes

Basic Sweet Cookie: 2 parts nuts to 1 part dried fruit (example: 2 cup pecans; 1 cup dates.) Add to this mixture any flavorings (i.e. vanilla, extracts, cinnamon, clove, pie spice, cardamom, ginger, lemon peel or something salty, etc.). For a crust it is recommended to reduce the dried fruit portion somewhat. A pie crust doesn't need to be as sweet because the filling is typically sweet. Soaking dried fruit before using it is also recommended. This makes it easier for the appliance to process it evenly.

Basic Sugar-Free Cookie: 4 cups soaked and dehydrated nuts, seeds OR sprouted grains; 1 tablespoon ground cinnamon, 10-15 drops liquid stevia extract, 4-5 tablespoons raw nut or seed butter (substitute water and 2 tsp. psyllium husks powder for this ingredient if using sprouted grains).

PROCEDURE

Smoother method (the fastest and easiest way): In a mixing bowl, combine all ingredients for the cookie/crust. Mix well. Using a food processor, process this mixture until it starts to come together and stick on the walls of the processor. Continue to process if you want all of the ingredients to be chopped more finely. Form into the desired cookie shape and refrigerate or dehydrate, OR press into a pie plate and dehydrate.

Smoothest method: In a mixing bowl, combine all ingredients for the cookie/crust. Mix well. Using the homogenizing (blank) attachment of an appropriate juicer, process this mixture. Be aware that in this procedure the juicer may get hot. To avoid cooking the mixture during this process, frequently check by feeling the juicer motor area and also the mixture that is being processed. Form into the desired cookie shape and refrigerate or dehydrate, OR press into a pie plate and dehydrate.

Smoothest Method:

COOKIE/PIE CRUST BASICS (continued)

PROCEDURE

Chunky method: Roughly
chop the nuts or seeds in a
food processor, according to
how chunky you want the
cookie/crust to be. Set aside in
a mixing bowl. Again in the
food processor, puree the dried
fruit and any other ingredients
you choose to use. Process
until a sticky paste is formed.
Add this mixture to the mixing bowl and combine it with
the chopped nuts/seeds by
hand. It should stick together
when pressed or squeezed into
a shape. Form into the desired
cookie shape and refrigerate or
dehydrate, OR press into a pie
plate and dehydrate.

Cookie Option 2

Cookie Option 3

MILK BASICS

Milks can be made from EITHER sprouted grains OR nuts/seeds blended with pure water and strained. The resulting milky liquid is typically white to off-white in color and can replace animal milk in conventional uses. It makes a very satisfying, nutrition-packed beverage.

See more information on Vita-Mix at end of book

USES FOR NUT & GRAIN MILKS

- beverage

- served with raw sprouted cereals

- base liquid for flavoring or making smoothies, dressings and/or soups

Basic Recipe

1 cup soaked nuts or seeds, or soaked grains
2 - 3 cups pure water

Add any other flavorings you like, for example vanilla, cinnamon, stevia, cardamom or nutmeg.

PROCEDURE

1. Blend the ingredients very well.

2. Strain through a sprout bag (a.k.a. nut-milk bag, this is ideal), or a very fine mesh strainer. Keep the pulp! What is left in the bag or strainer is known as the "meal" or pulp. We dehydrate this and use it for other things, such as cookies, crusts, patés, and cheeses. Anytime you see a recipe that calls for almond meal or some other nut or seed meal, this is what the recipe is referring to. Nut milk only lasts 1-2 days in refrigeration, so drink up!

DEHYDRATION BASICS

The process of removing water from food.
Dehydration can be accomplished by drying in the sun (commonly referred to as 'sun-dried'), or with the help of a food dehydrator. A food dehydrator typically has a heating element and a fan that circulates the warm air. Dehydration was created as a way to preserve food by lowering its moisture content, thereby slowing bacterial growth and curtailing spoilage. In raw food preparation, however, dehydration is typically used as a way to add variety to the diet. A dehydrator is not absolutely necessary, but from our experience it helps people stay on this healthy, raw food based program. Using it, one can create lots of crunchy treats like chips, crackers, cookies and fruit snacks. Other creative uncooked dishes that may be enhanced by dehydrating include stuffed mushrooms, pizza, burgers, cakes and pies.

USES FOR DEHYDRATION

• snack foods—crunchy nuts, seeds and veggies, cookies, crackers, veggie chips and pizza

• food preservation

• adding "cooked" appeal without cooking

• making travel food, fruit leather, burgers and nut loaves

OTHER BASICS

TEMPERATURE
Always dehydrate at or below 115° F or 42° C to avoid further enzyme loss. A dehydrator with temperature control is essential.

CAN YOU USE YOUR CONVENTIONAL OVEN?
This is not recommended for two reasons. First, most conventional ovens do not have a temperature setting low enough to preserve enzymes (lower than 115° F). Even the warm setting is typically too hot. Secondly, conventional ovens have no circulating air or moisture escape, which extends the drying time significantly and lessens the chance of having even temperature distribution. If you have a convection oven (one which has a fan), and you are certain that the temperature stays low enough, it may work as a dehydrator. Be certain to check the air temperature periodically, even if you are using a regular dehydrator, just to be sure that the gauges are accurate.

DEHYDRATION TIMES
Times will vary depending on the thickness of what you are dehydrating, how full the dehydrator is, and the moisture in the air and in the foods you are drying. We cannot say exactly how long it will take foods to dry; this is why most charts in books provide a range of times. Some foods are better when they are totally dry, whereas others are better only somewhat dry, or slightly warm. You will become accustomed to knowing when something is "done" after you have experimented with dehydrating. A good indicator of dryness is to open or break apart the food item and see if it is darker in the center, or if it is still wet. Try tasting the item. When dehydrating at the temperatures we suggest, you can't burn anything so don't worry too much about the timing. Most items take at least overnight and some may take up to three days. Dehydrating is much slower than baking. Patience is the key.

STORING

Store dehydrated items that have been completely dried in airtight bags, jars, or containers and keep them at room temperature. If you plan on keeping things more than one month, keep them in a very cool place or refrigerate them to prevent any rancidity. *Always refrigerate partially dehydrated items.*

A KEY POINT

Dehydrated food is similar to cooked food in that it lacks the high water content of fresh foods. While dehydrated food is obviously not as alive and vivacious as fresh produce, it is still much better than cooked food. It possesses enough enzymes so that it will not tax your body when being digested. It is easiest on the digestive system to consume dehydrated food with other foods that have higher water content. For example, eat dehydrated crackers with a salad or crumble them over the top of the salad. These healthy prepared foods look, taste and feel like cooked foods, and will encourage you to maintain your life-giving diet. If you eat an excess of dehydrated food, you may experience a feeling of being "blocked up" or heavy inside, due to concentrated state of the food and the lack of moisture. For best results, make sure that you maintain adequate hydration, especially when eating dehydrated foods.

FOR STICKY/WET ITEMS

Use either a non-toxic teflex sheet (available from the Hippocrates Store: www.HippocratesInstitute.org or 561.471.8876) or unbleached parchment paper to cover the mesh screen of the tray. This will prevent dripping and sticking. Teflex sheets are preferred because they are reusable.

D This symbol means the recipe is dehydrated or can be easily modified for dehydration. See the Dehydrate Chapter of this book, pages 112-119, for additional recipes and instructions.

DEHYDRATION BASICS (continued)

Basic Recipes

Fruit Leather: To make fruit leather, first choose a fruit or combination of fruits to use. Some examples are banana, strawberry, peach, nectarine, mango, papaya, kiwi, apple, pear, cherry, blueberry, plum, fig, star fruit, pineapple, and berry. Blend the fruit into a puree. For every one-cup of fruit puree, add 1 tsp. psyllium powder or ground flax seed and blend well. This will cause the puree to become very thick and gooey. Allow the blended puree to stand and thicken at least 30 minutes. Blend again and then pour onto a dehydrator tray covered with a teflex sheet or unbleached parchment paper. Pour the mixture on thick and allow it to stay that way. Dehydrate until desired stickiness and chewiness is achieved. You will most likely need to flip the leather midway through so that it will dry evenly. At that time, you can remove the teflex. Store fruit leather in a sealed bag or roll it up with "healthy" plastic wrap from the health food store to prevent self-sticking.

Fruit Chips/Pieces (for the athletic and healthy, disease-free person): To dehydrate your own fruit, first choose which fruit you wish to use. Some fruits that dehydrate well are apples, bananas, pears, mango, papaya, berries, and peaches. Dehydrated fruit is very concentrated in sugar, so it is important to consume small amounts and only if you are healthy. Use different flavorings (which are also optional) such as vanilla, cinnamon, orange, mint, etc. Place the slices on a dehydrator tray and dehydrate until crunchy or chewy, whichever you desire.

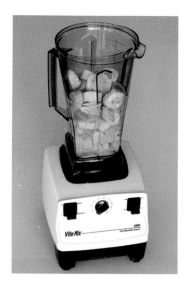

Vegetable Chips: Choose your favorite vegetables. Some examples are zucchini, yellow squash, sweet potato, carrot, beet, radish, turnips, celery root, and even cucumbers. Slice the starchier, denser vegetables into approximately 1/16 inch thick slices. Slice the more watery vegetables into approximately 1/8 inch thick slices. To add a little something special to the chips, marinate them in herbs, spices and Bragg Liquid Aminos or Nama Shoyu for at least 30 minutes. Ideas for flavorings include: garlic powder, chili powder, cayenne pepper, pizza seasoning, paprika, Mexican seasoning, Cajun seasoning, rosemary, oregano, and thyme. Place the slices on a dehydrator tray and dehydrate until crunchy. Some vegetables will get crunchier than others. Experiment to see which ones you like best.

D Stuffed Mushrooms:
These can be made without any dehydration, but if you want a more "cooked" appeal to them, dehydration is the way to go. Use whole portobello caps, crimini caps, or even shiitake caps. Marinate mushrooms for at least 30 minutes in Bragg Liquid Aminos or Nama Shoyu and any other flavorings you prefer. Drain off the liquid. Stuff the mushroom caps, upside down, with your favorite paté or thick dip. Dehydrate overnight. Serve. You may dehydrate them further for a very crunchy and chewy snack. See page 84 for complete recipe.

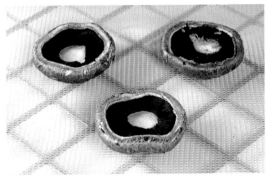

DEHYDRATION

Basic Recipes

Grain Crackers: These easy, high energy crackers can be made most simply with any sprouted grain and water. Additional vegetables add great flavor and lighten the texture of grain crackers. To make the crackers, first combine all cracker ingredients in a mixing bowl, then blend ingredients together. Note: Blend the ingredients with just enough pure water to achieve a thick batter. You may need to process small batches at a time to maintain its thickness. Spread this mixture evenly on a dehydrator tray, scoring lines where you want the crackers to break apart. Dehydrate overnight, flip and remove the teflex sheet. Dehydrate again until desired dryness is achieved.

Savory Crackers: A great place to start is with this ratio: 1 part nuts/seeds (soaked): 1 part fresh vegetables (by volume). Combine these in a bowl (roughly chop the vegetables) and add any other flavorings, seasonings, herbs, etc. that you like. Toss together. Use the homogenizing attachment of an appropriate juicer (for a very smooth mixture) or the S-blade of a food processor to mash the mixture. Spread evenly on a dehydrator tray and mark lines to "cut" the crackers. You can also form them individually into shapes. Dehydrate overnight, flip and remove the teflex sheet. Dehydrate again at least for the remainder of the day or until desired dryness is achieved.

Flax Crackers: The simplest and most economical cracker there is! A very basic and very good recipe to start from is: 4 cups flax seeds (½ ground in a spice grinder or blender, ½ whole), 4 cups water, juice of one lemon, and your choice of flavor enhancer, to taste. Mix all ingredients in a bowl and season to taste. Let stand for at least 30 minutes to gel. Spread a thin layer of this mixture on a dehydrator tray using a sheet beneath. If your mixture is thick enough, you can score or "cut" the crackers. Otherwise just break the cracker sheet into pieces when it is dry. Dehydrate overnight, flip and remove the sheet, and dehydrate for the remainder of the day if necessary.

Sweet Cookies: See the Cookie/Pie Crusts basics section on page 32.

Other Dried Veggies & Salads: Dehydration is a great way to preserve food so that it does not go to waste. Most any fruit or vegetable can be dehydrated, but not all are suitable for chips. Some just turn out better than others. Most popular dehydrates include dulse, bell peppers, carrots, onions, and greens, such as kale, collards, and chard. You can also make many of the salads in this book without the oil and then dehydrate them for great travel food! Use these random dehydrated salad pieces to make your own seasonings by grinding them up in a spice grinder or blender.

The following foods do not do well because of their fat content: avocado, olives, any salad with oil on it and thick rich sauces, like those made of pine or macadamia nuts. Whole sprouted grains or beans are like rocks when dehydrated whole, but you can blend them and then dehydrate them.

DEHYDRATION (continued)

Basic Recipes

Pizza Crust: Pizza crust can be made by forming and dehydrating any paté, grain cracker batter, or other cracker mixture into individual pizza rounds or large pan pizza size rounds. Here is one of the many recipes for a pizza crust: 1 cup sunflower seeds, soaked & dehydrated; 1 cup almond meal; 1 cup pumpkin seeds, soaked & dehydrated; ¾ cup flax seeds (ground); 2 tsp. psyllium husks powder; 3 teaspoons Herbs De Provence; 10 drops liquid stevia extract, 2 tablespoons Nama Shoyu or Bragg Liquid Aminos; 1⅔ cups water; 1 clove garlic.

In a food processor, combine nuts/seeds, psyllium and dried herbs. Process until a fine crumble is achieved. Add remaining ingredients and process well. The mixture will come together as a slightly sticky dough. By hand, take the mixture and form it into a large ball. Using a teflex sheet or unbleached parchment paper beneath, place the dough ball on a dehydrator tray. Smooth out to form a large round, leaving the edges raised as the crust. Dehydrate overnight. Flip and dehydrate for the remainder of the day. Make a wonderful raw pizza sauce and top with your choice of vegetables and herbs, then dehydrate again overnight (optional).

Nut/Seeds: Soak nuts/seeds overnight in pure water. Drain off the water and rinse the nuts/seeds. Spread them evenly on dehydrator trays. To create seasoned nuts/seeds, toss them with your favorite spices and seasonings after draining the water. You can flavor them in hundreds of ways, from simple Bragg Liquid Aminos and cayenne to Mexican or curry flavored. Then spread the nuts/seeds on a dehydrator tray and dehydrate. Soaking and dehydrating could take more than 10 hours, so it's a great idea to stock your cupboard with several varieties of soaked and dehydrated nuts and seeds in advance. That way, when you want to make something or are just feeling creative, you are already prepared.

PROCEDURE

Dehydration varies for each individual item. Refer to the guidelines under the definition of dehydrating and each individual recipe.

READING RECIPES

Recipes complement the basic procedures outlined in the beginning of this book. Recipes are meant to be used as guidelines. Please do not feel constrained by them. If an ingredient is used that you do not care for, simply make a substitution or leave it out. Living food preparation is very simple and any recipe can be easily modified and still be excellent. You will get the best results by familiarizing yourself with all the procedures of a recipe prior to making it.

It's a good idea to taste your preparations before declaring them complete. You can always add and change a recipe to make it something that you very much enjoy, even if at first it doesn't please your taste buds. The taste and freshness of produce, origin of produce and your own taste differences from the recipe author's affect how the food tastes to you. So feel free to season your food to your liking to ensure the most enjoyable meal every time!

Remember…sprouts should be at the heart of every meal!

HOW TO READ THE RECIPES

Ingredient Measurements:
1 tablespoon = ½ oz
3 teaspoons = 1 tablespoon
1 cup = 8 oz.
oz = ounce
lb = pound

Metric conversions:
1 tablespoon = 15 milliliters
1 teaspoon = 5 milliliters
1 cup = 250 milliliters
1 oz = 28.35 grams
16 oz = .47 liters
1 lb = .45 kilogram

Ingredient cuts:
julienne = long, thin, matchstick cut
dice = square cut
chiffonnade = thin, ribbon-like cut
slice = straight cut against the grain

Important: If a preparation process appears in an ingredient line prior to a food item—for example: 1 cup soaked dates—measure 1 cup of dates that have ALREADY been soaked. If a preparation process appears in an ingredient line after the food item (separated by a comma)—for example: 1 cup dates, soaked—measure the 1 cup of dates BEFORE soaking them. This rule applies to all preparation processes, i.e., dehydrated, chopped, diced, etc.

A few of the recipes contain foods that we at Hippocrates do not recommend. In these recipes we have recommended alternatives in the *"How to Hippocratize these recipes."*

 This symbol indicates a recipe provided by Guest Chef **Chad Sarno**.

D This symbol means the recipe is dehydrated or can be easily modified for dehydration. See the Dehydrate Chapter of this book, pages 112-119, for additional recipes and instructions.

Broccoli *with* Pine Nut Ranch Dressing

Dressings and Sauces

CHAPTER 4

MOST PEOPLE LOVE DRESSINGS AND SAUCES. A good dressing can jazz up any food, especially ones that are very good for you and that you want to incorporate into your new diet. It is helpful as you adopt raw foods to use and enjoy these delicious dressings. As your palate cleanses and taste buds awaken, you will find that you wish to eat foods in their natural state, so making your own dressings is a great way to start learning about raw food preparation. All you need is a blender and five minutes.

Your dressings and sauces should complement the foods that you are dressing, with respect to the laws of food combining. (See the Food Combining section on pages 15-17 for more information.)

Most dressings will last 3-4 days in refrigeration. Anything that is blended should be used immediately for its optimum nutritional value as well as flavor. Avocado-based dressings are one-day dressings. For more on the basics of dressings, see the Blending section pages 20-25 under Basic Procedures.

Celery Dulse Dressing

YIELD: 2 CUPS

2 cups chopped celery
½ cup dulse seaweed, snipped into pieces
1 clove garlic
½ cup extra virgin olive oil
½ cup water or vegetable juice
1 tablespoon fresh lemon juice
cayenne to taste, optional

In a blender, combine all ingredients. Blend well and season to taste.

Several recipes throughout the book include dressings and sauces created especially for a featured dish. These recipes may provide you with additional inspiration. Enjoy!

Almond Ginger Dressing

YIELD: 4 CUPS

2 cups chopped bell pepper
1 cup raw almond butter
½ cup chopped scallion
¼ cup chopped red beet
2 tablespoons chopped ginger
1 clove garlic
½ teaspoon ground cinnamon

¼ teaspoon ground clove
1 cup water
1 tablespoon Bragg Liquid Aminos
   or Nama Shoyu
½ tablespoon alcohol-free vanilla extract
½ tablespoon fresh lemon juice, optional
¼ teaspoon liquid stevia extract

In a blender, combine all ingredients. Blend well and season to taste.

Variations:
Add 1 tablespoon ground hijiki (grind in a spice grinder or blender) and ¼ teaspoon cayenne pepper for a great Pad Thai sauce. For an excellent creamy curry sauce, add 1 tablespoon curry powder.

Broccoli Dill Dressing

YIELD: 2½ CUPS

2 cups chopped broccoli stems
½ cup chopped celery
½ cup chopped fresh dill
1 clove garlic
1 teaspoon kelp powder

½ cup water or celery juice
½ cup extra virgin olive oil
2 teaspoons fresh lemon juice, optional
1 teaspoon Bragg Liquid Aminos or
   Nama Shoyu, optional

In a blender, combine all ingredients. Blend well and season to taste.

Option: Substitute basil for dill for a Brocco-Basil Dressing.

Tarragon Mustard Dressing

YIELD: 3 CUPS

1 cup chopped zucchini
½ cup chopped celery
¼ cup chopped red onion
1 clove garlic
2½ tablespoons dried tarragon
1½ teaspoons ground mustard seed
½ cup water or Hippocrates Green Juice*

⅓ cup extra virgin olive oil
1 tablespoon fresh lemon or
   sauerkraut juice, optional
3 drops liquid stevia extract
Bragg Liquid Aminos, dulse,
   or kelp granules to taste, optional

In a blender, combine all ingredients. Blend well and season to taste.

* See page 20 for Hippocrates Green Juice recipe.

Russian Dressing

YIELD: 2½ CUPS

1 cup chopped red bell pepper
½ cup chopped celery
½ cup chopped fresh dill
¼ cup chopped red onion
1 tablespoon dried tarragon
1 teaspoon caraway seed
1 teaspoon kelp powder

½ teaspoon garlic powder
½ cup extra virgin olive oil
½ cup water
2 teaspoons fresh lemon juice, optional
¼ teaspoon liquid stevia extract
½ cup finely diced cucumber

In a blender, combine all ingredients except the cucumber. Blend well and season to taste. Stir in the cucumber and serve.

Sunny Onion Dressing Ⓓ

YIELD: 2 CUPS

1 cup sunflower seeds, soaked
½ cup chopped red onion
½ cup chopped fresh herbs of your choice
1 clove garlic

1 cup water
2 tablespoons fresh lemon juice, optional
Bragg Liquid Aminos, dulse
    or kelp granules to taste, optional

In a blender, combine all ingredients. Blend well and season to taste.

Avo-Parsley Dressing

YIELD: 2 CUPS

1 cup chopped fresh parsley
½ avocado
¼ cup chopped red onion
1 clove garlic

2 tablespoons dulse flakes
1 - 1¼ cups water or cucumber juice
1 tablespoon fresh lemon juice, optional

In a blender, combine all ingredients. Blend well and season to taste.

Lemon Dulse Dressing

YIELD: 1¼ CUPS

1 cup whole leaf dulse, snipped into pieces
1 clove garlic
¼ teaspoon cayenne

½ cup water
½ cup extra virgin olive oil
3 tablespoons fresh lemon juice, optional

In a blender, combine all ingredients. Blend well and season to taste.

SIMPLE CAESAR SALAD WITH WHOLE LEAF DULSE
AND ROSEMARY CROUTONS

Simple Caesar Salad

Serves 4

1 handful of chopped romaine
2+ ounces Caesar dressing (see recipe below)
1 tablespoon shaved nori

¼ cup Rosemary Croutons (see recipe below)
Squirt of olive oil
Freshly cracked black pepper to taste[1]

1. In a mixing bowl, toss the romaine, Caesar dressing, dulse, croutons, olive oil, and cracked black pepper well, dispersing the dressing equally.

2. Center all salad in bowl and top with pine nut parmesan.

How to "Hippocratize" this recipe
[1] Substitute cayenne pepper for black pepper, or omit pepper entirely.

Rosemary Garlic Croutons ⓓ
(or Veggie Flax Crackers)

Yields 8-9 dehydrator trays

2 cups golden flax seeds, soaked in 3 cups
  water for 4-6 hours
2 cups sunflower seeds (or almonds),
  soaked in water for 6-8 hours
3 carrots, chopped
2 cups celery, chopped
⅓ cup leek, chopped
1 cup red bell pepper, chopped

3 tablespoons rosemary, dried
2 tablespoons garlic powder or
  3 cloves fresh garlic
2 tablespoons Italian seasoning, dried
½ teaspoon cayenne
1½ tablespoons Celtic sea salt[1]
Freshly cracked black pepper to taste[2]

1. In a food processor, blend the soaked flax and sunflower seeds until the mixture forms into a pâté; there should be very few whole flax seeds. Place in large mixing bowl; set aside.

2. Process the remaining ingredients until finely minced or blended to a smooth consistency. Add to flax batch and mix thoroughly. Tip: mixing with your hands is much more effective than using a spoon.

3. Using a spatula spread a ½-inch even layer on each teflex sheet. When evenly spread, score 16 x 16, or increase the number of scores for smaller croutons.

4. Place in dehydrator and dehydrate at 110 degrees for 12 - 16 hours.**

5. Serve with Caesar salad and as an extra.

** **Important!** Halfway through the drying process, flip the teflex sheets onto the screens and peel them away; this will allow the underside of the food to dry thoroughly. Separate the croutons and continue drying until crunchy.

How to "Hippocratize" this recipe:

[1] Substitute dulse, Bragg Liquid Aminos, Nama Shoyu, kelp powder or celery powder for the Celtic sea salt.

[2] Substitute cayenne pepper for black pepper, or omit pepper entirely.

Vegan Caesar Dressing

Yield: 3 Cups

1½ cup olive oil
6 cloves garlic
5 stalks celery, chopped
3 tablespoons white miso[1]
½ cup lemon juice

1½ cup water
8 dates, pitted[2]
¼ cup Nama Shoyu
1½ tablespoons sea salt[3]
¼ cup kelp granules

Place all ingredients in a blender and blend until smooth. Adjust water for desired thickness. Dressing will last up to 5 days in refrigerator.

How to "Hippocratize" this recipe:

[1] Instead of miso, use more Nama Shoyu if necessary.

[2] Substitute stevia (to taste) for the dates.

[3] Substitute dulse, Bragg Liquid Aminos, Nama Shoyu, kelp powder or celery powder for the Celtic sea salt.

Hot Mustard Sauce

YIELD: 1 CUP

½ cup freshly ground mustard seed
1 tablespoon ground flax seed
½ teaspoon ground turmeric
½ - ¾ cup water

¼ cup extra virgin olive oil
1½ tablespoons fresh lemon juice, optional
1 tablespoon flax oil
1 tablespoon Bragg Liquid Aminos

In a blender, combine all ingredients. Blend until smooth. Season to taste.

Carrot Tahini Dressing

YIELD: 3½ CUPS

1 cup raw sesame tahini
½ cup chopped scallion
¼ cup chopped fresh dill
1 clove garlic
½ tablespoon dried oregano
1 ½ cups fresh carrot juice

⅓ cup fresh celery juice
1 tablespoon fresh lemon juice, optional
½ tablespoon Bragg Liquid Aminos
  or Nama Shoyu
⅛ teaspoon liquid stevia extract
½ cup chopped fresh dill

In a blender, combine all ingredients except the ½ cup chopped fresh dill. Blend well and season to taste. Stir in the dill. Serve.

Caesar Dressing II

YIELD: 1½ CUPS

½ cup raw sesame tahini
¼ cup Hijiki, soaked in water
1 clove garlic
2 tablespoons dulse flakes
½ teaspoon mustard powder

⅔ cup water
⅛ cup extra virgin olive oil
1 tablespoon fresh lemon juice, optional
1 tablespoon Bragg Liquid Aminos
  or Nama Shoyu

In a blender, combine all ingredients. Blend well and season to taste.

Creamy Dill Spinach Dressing

YIELD: 2 CUPS

2 cups spinach, packed
1 small avocado or ½ large avocado
1 cup chopped fresh dill
1 clove garlic

1 teaspoon kelp powder or
  Bragg Liquid Aminos
1½ cups water or cucumber juice
1½ tablespoons fresh lemon juice, optional

In a blender, combine all ingredients. Blend well and season to taste.

Cosmic Cumin Dressing

YIELD: 2 CUPS

1 cup chopped yellow squash
¼ cup chopped scallion
1 clove garlic
2 teaspoons ground cumin
1 teaspoon kelp powder

½ cup raw sesame oil
½ cup water
1½ tablespoons fresh lemon juice, optional
2 drops liquid stevia extract

In a blender, combine all ingredients. Blend well and season to taste.

Spinach Tahini Dressing

YIELD: 3 CUPS

3 cups chopped spinach
1 cup chopped fresh basil
½ cup chopped celery
½ cup raw sesame tahini
⅓ cup chopped red onion
¼ cup fresh oregano leaves

2 cloves garlic
1 tablespoon Frontier Pizza Seasoning
1 cup celery juice
1 teaspoon fresh lemon juice, optional
1 teaspoon Bragg Liquid Aminos
   or Nama Shoyu

In a blender, combine all ingredients. Blend well and season to taste.

Pine Nut Ranch Dressing

YIELD: 2 CUPS

1 cup pine nuts, soaked
⅓ cup chopped celery
¼ cup chopped red onion
1 clove garlic
1 tablespoon Frontier Pizza Seasoning

1 teaspoon kelp powder
1 cup water or vegetable juice*
½ teaspoon Bragg Liquid Aminos
   or Nama Shoyu
¼ teaspoon liquid stevia extract

In a blender, combine all ingredients. Blend well and season to taste.

* See page 20 for information on basic vegetable juice.

Sweet Potato Curry Sauce

YIELD: 3 CUPS

2 cups chopped sweet potato
¼ cup chopped scallion
1 tablespoon curry powder
½ teaspoon ground cinnamon
1½ cups water
½ cup raw sesame oil

1 tablespoon fresh lemon juice, optional
½ teaspoon Bragg Liquid Aminos
   or Nama Shoyu
¼ teaspoon liquid stevia extract
½ cup chopped fresh basil
½ cup chopped fresh cilantro

In a blender, combine all ingredients. Blend well and season to taste. Stir in basil and cilantro if desired.

Pesto Dressing

YIELD: 1½ CUPS

1 cup chopped fresh parsley
1 cup chopped basil
½ cup pine nuts, soaked
¼ cup chopped fresh oregano
1 clove garlic

1 teaspoon kelp powder
⅔ - ¾ cup water
2 tablespoons extra virgin olive oil
2 tablespoons fresh lemon juice, optional

In a blender, combine all ingredients. Blend well and season to taste.

Fiesta Dressing

YIELD: 2 CUPS

1 cup chopped red bell pepper
½ avocado
⅓ cup chopped celery
¼ cup chopped scallion
¼ cup chopped fresh cilantro
1 clove garlic

1 tablespoon chili powder
1 teaspoon kelp powder
¼ teaspoon cayenne
1 cup water or carrot juice
1½ tablespoons fresh lemon juice, optional
⅛ teaspoon liquid stevia extract

In a blender, combine all ingredients and blend until very smooth. Use water or cucumber juice to thin, or avocado if necessary to thicken. Season to taste and serve.

Avo Mayo

YIELD: 1½ CUPS

2 avocados
2 cloves garlic, chopped
½ teaspoon ground mustard seed
¼ teaspoon cayenne, optional
¼ cup extra virgin olive oil

¼ cup fresh lemon juice, optional
1 teaspoon Bragg Liquid Aminos
  or Nama Shoyu
⅛ teaspoon liquid stevia extract

In a food processor or strong blender, combine all ingredients. Mix well and season to taste.

Note: Tangy and rich! The only way you know it isn't "real" mayonnaise is by the color. Use sparingly.

Red Pepper Ketchup

YIELD: 2 CUPS

2 cups chopped red bell pepper
¼ cup chopped red onion
⅛ cup chopped red beet
2 tablespoons paprika
2 tablespoons ground flax seed
1 tablespoon celery powder*

2 teaspoons garlic powder
1 pinch ground clove
⅔ cup extra virgin olive oil
1½ tablespoons fresh lemon juice, optional
¼ teaspoon liquid stevia extract

In a blender, combine all ingredients. Blend well and season to taste.

* Celery powder or "Celery Salt" is made by dehydrating celery, then grinding it to a powder using a spice grinder or dry blender. See page 113 for recipe.

Raw Red Pepper Marinara

YIELD: 4 CUPS

4 chopped red bell peppers
½ red onion, roughly chopped
1 bunch fresh basil, chopped
1 clove garlic
1 tablespoon Frontier Pizza Seasoning
¼ cup extra virgin olive oil

1 teaspoon fresh lemon juice, optional
fresh oregano to taste
fresh thyme to taste
Bragg Liquid Aminos, dulse,
   or kelp granules to taste, optional
liquid stevia extract to taste

In a food processor, combine all ingredients and process. Season to taste. If a thicker sauce is desired, add 1 teaspoon psyllium husks powder.

Note: This sauce is perfect for raw pasta (Spiraghetti). If you are using it to make raw pizza, we recommend blending it to a smoother consistency.

Sesame Ginger Dressing

YIELD: 3 CUPS

⅓ cup chopped scallion
⅓ cup sliced ginger root
1 clove garlic
1¼ cups raw sesame oil
¾ cup flax seed oil
⅓ cup fresh lemon juice, optional

¼ cup Bragg Liquid Aminos
   or Nama Shoyu
¾ teaspoon ground mustard seed
¼ teaspoon liquid stevia extract
¼ teaspoon cayenne, optional

In a blender, combine all ingredients. Blend well and season to taste. This dressing will last at least 1 week in refrigeration and makes a great marinade for any salad.

Red Pepper Corn Salsa

YIELD: 3 CUPS

2 cups chopped red bell pepper
½ red onion, chopped
1 cup fresh corn
½ cup shredded carrot
⅓ cup finely sliced scallion
2 avocados, diced into small pieces

½ - 1 cup chopped fresh cilantro
1 teaspoon kelp powder
cayenne to taste
1½ tablespoons fresh lemon juice, optional
1 tablespoon extra virgin olive oil

1. In a food processor, using the pulse function or simply turning the processor on and off quickly, chop the red bell pepper until you have a juicy, finely chopped, salsa-like mixture. Set aside in a mixing bowl.

2. Chop the red onion the same way. Add to the mixing bowl with the red bell pepper.

3. Add remaining ingredients to the mixing bowl. Stir to combine well. Season to taste and serve.

Note: This mixture goes especially well with flax crackers and/or vegetable chips (vegetable slices raw or dehydrated).

Red Pepper Italian Dressing

YIELD: 4 CUPS

2 cups chopped red bell pepper
1 cup chopped carrot
½ cup chopped red onion
2 cloves garlic
1 tablespoon dried onion flakes
1 tablespoon Frontier Pizza Seasoning
½ teaspoon garlic powder

1 cup extra virgin olive oil
½ cup water or celery juice
1 tablespoon fresh lemon juice, optional
½ tablespoon Bragg Liquid Aminos
   or Nama Shoyu
⅛ teaspoon liquid stevia extract

In a blender, combine all ingredients. Blend well and season to taste.

Carrot Avocado Dill Dressing

YIELD: 1½ CUPS

½ avocado
⅓ cup chopped fresh dill
1 clove garlic
cayenne to taste, optional
1 cup carrot juice

½ cup celery juice
¼ cup water, if needed
1 teaspoon fresh lemon juice, optional
¼ cup chopped scallion

In a blender, combine all ingredients except the scallion. Blend well. Stir in the scallion. Season to taste.

French-Style Dressing

YIELD: 2 CUPS

1 cup chopped red bell pepper
½ cup pine nuts, soaked
½ cup carrot juice
¼ teaspoon ground clove
⅓ cup water

1 tablespoon fresh lemon juice, optional
1 teaspoon Bragg Liquid Aminos
   or Nama Shoyu
¼ teaspoon liquid stevia extract

In a blender, combine all ingredients. Blend well and season to taste.

Cucumber Dill Dressing

YIELD: 2½ CUPS

2 cups chopped cucumber
1 cup chopped fresh dill
¼ cup chopped red onion
1 clove garlic

½ tablespoon kelp powder
¼ teaspoon cayenne
½ cup extra virgin olive oil
1 tablespoon fresh lemon juice, optional

In a blender, combine all ingredients. Blend well and season to taste.

Gingered Pumpkin Seed Dressing

YIELD: 2½ CUPS

1 cup pumpkin seeds, soaked, or
¾ cup pumpkin seed butter
1 cup chopped broccoli stems
2 tablespoons chopped ginger
1 clove garlic

1⅓ cups water or celery juice
¾ tablespoon Bragg Liquid Aminos
   or Nama Shoyu
1½ teaspoons fresh lemon juice, optional
¼ teaspoon liquid stevia extract

In a blender, combine all ingredients. Blend well and season to taste.

Southwestern Dressing

YIELD: 2½ CUPS

2 cups chopped yellow squash
⅓ cup chopped onion
⅓ cup chopped celery
⅓ cup chopped bell pepper
1 clove garlic
1½ tablespoons chili powder
1 teaspoon dried oregano

⅛ teaspoon cayenne
½ cup extra virgin olive oil
½ cup water or vegetable juice*
1 tablespoon fresh lemon juice, optional
¾ tablespoon Bragg Liquid Aminos
   or Nama Shoyu, optional
⅛ teaspoon liquid stevia extract

In a blender, combine all ingredients. Blend well and season to taste.

* See page 20 for information on basic vegetable juice.

Red Pepper Tahini Dressing

YIELD: 3 CUPS

2 red bell peppers, roughly chopped
1 cup raw sesame tahini
1 - 2 cloves garlic
1 tablespoon Frontier Pizza Seasoning
1 cup water

1 tablespoon fresh lemon juice, optional
¼ cup dehydrated bell pepper, or
2 drops liquid stevia extract
Bragg Liquid Aminos, dulse,
   or kelp granules to taste, optional

In a blender, combine all ingredients. Blend well and season to taste.
Add water to adjust consistency.

Red Pepper Sunflower Sauce

YIELD: 1½ CUPS

1 cup chopped red bell pepper
1 cup sunflower seeds, soaked
1 clove garlic
1 tablespoon paprika
1 tablespoon dried oregano

½ cup water or vegetable juice*
1 tablespoon Bragg Liquid Aminos
   or Nama Shoyu
1 teaspoon fresh lemon juice, optional
3 - 4 drops liquid stevia extract

In a blender, combine all ingredients. Blend well and season to taste.

* See page 20 for information on basic vegetable juice.

Asian Carrot Pine Nut Dressing

YIELD: 2½ CUPS

1 cup pine nuts, soaked
1 tablespoon chopped fresh ginger
1 clove garlic
1 cup carrot juice
½ cup bell pepper juice

2 teaspoons fresh lemon juice, optional
½ tablespoon Bragg Liquid Aminos
   or Nama Shoyu
¼ cup finely chopped scallion

In a blender, combine all ingredients except the chopped scallion. Blend well and season to taste. Stir in the scallion. Serve.

Macadamia Nut Alfredo Sauce

YIELD: 4 CUPS

2 cups macadamia nuts, soaked
1 clove garlic
1 pinch ground nutmeg
2 cups water
¾ cup extra virgin olive oil

1 lemon, juiced
⅛ teaspoon liquid stevia extract
Nama Shoyu to taste, optional
1 cup almond meal, optional

In a blender, combine all ingredients except the almond meal. Blend well and season to taste. Stir in the almond meal (optional) for a parmesan cheese-like effect.

* Almond meal is the dehydrated pulp strained out when making almond milk.
  Note: An excellent but very rich sauce; use only occasionally.

Zucchini Pine Nut Sauce

YIELD: 2½ CUPS

1 cup chopped zucchini
1 cup pine nuts, soaked
½ cup chopped fresh dill
1 clove garlic
1½ cups water or vegetable juice*

½ tablespoon fresh lemon juice, optional
1 teaspoon Bragg Liquid Aminos
   or Nama Shoyu
⅛ teaspoon liquid stevia extract

In a blender, combine all ingredients. Blend well and season to taste.

* See page 20 for information on basic vegetable juice.

Lemon Tahini Dressing

YIELD: 2 CUPS

1 cup chopped cucumber
½ cup raw sesame tahini
¼ cup chopped scallion
1 clove garlic
1 teaspoon kelp powder

cayenne to taste
½ cup water or vegetable juice*
3½ tablespoons fresh lemon juice
3 - 4 drops liquid stevia extract

In a blender, combine all ingredients. Blend well and season to taste.

* See page 20 for information on basic vegetable juice.

Hot Sauce

YIELD: 3 CUPS

1½ cups chopped red bell pepper
1 chopped cherry bomb hot pepper
1 teaspoon paprika
1 teaspoon chili powder
½ teaspoon garlic powder

½ teaspoon kelp powder
¼ teaspoon cayenne
3 tablespoons extra virgin olive oil
½ tablespoon fresh lemon juice, optional
¼ teaspoon liquid stevia extract

In a blender, combine all ingredients. Blend well and season to taste.

Hippocrates House Dressing

YIELD: 1½ CUPS

1 cup high quality plant oil*
2¼ tablespoons fresh lemon juice, optional
2½ tablespoons Bragg Liquid Aminos
   or Nama Shoyu

2 cloves garlic
2 teaspoons ground mustard seed
¼ teaspoon cayenne

In a blender, combine all ingredients. Blend well, add 2-4 tablespoons water as you blend.
Season to taste.

* Use one or a blend of either extra virgin olive oil, raw sesame oil, raw pumpkin seed oil, flax oil,
   and/or hempseed oil.

Soups

CHAPTER 5

LIVE SOUPS ARE AN EXCELLENT WAY to make a quick meal that is easy to digest. They also provide a satisfying change of texture. Many people enjoy raw soups with dehydrated crackers. This is a wise way to consume dehydrated foods because you are eating them with a very watery entrée. Like dressings, the simplest raw soups take only five minutes to prepare. In fact, a dressing recipe is a good base for making a soup. But remember to reduce the quantity of fat, especially if it is oil. And don't forget to "chew" your raw soups, to mix them with the enzymes in your mouth. It is always best to consume raw soups immediately for optimal nutrition, energy and the freshest flavors.

Adzuki Chili

YIELD: 3 CUPS

1 cup sprouted adzuki beans
½ cup chopped celery
½ cup finely chopped red bell pepper, chopped in food processor
½ cup chopped fresh cilantro
½ cup whole leaf dulse, snipped into pieces
¼ cup finely diced red onion

1. In a mixing bowl, combine the 1 cup adzuki beans, celery, ½ cup red bell pepper, cilantro, dulse, and red onion.

2. In a blender, combine the sauce ingredients. Blend well and season to taste.

3. Combine the sauce and bean mixture. Allow to marinate overnight and serve.

Sauce:
1 cup chopped red bell pepper
¼ cup sprouted adzuki beans
¼ cup chopped scallion
1 teaspoon chili powder
½ teaspoon onion powder
½ teaspoon dried oregano
½ teaspoon kelp powder
cayenne to taste
½ cup water
¼ cup extra virgin olive oil
1 - 2 tablespoons fresh lemon juice, optional
1 tablespoon Bragg Liquid Aminos or Nama Shoyu
⅛ teaspoon liquid stevia extract

Cool Cucumber Soup

YIELD: 2 SERVINGS

1 cup cucumber, chopped
2 cups nut or seed milk
2 tablespoons scallion, thinly sliced

8 - 12 cucumber slices
¼ cup fresh chives, finely chopped
1 tablespoon kelp powder

Add Almonds

In a blender, combine the 1 cup cucumber and nut/seed milk. Blend until smooth. Stir in the scallion and cucumber slices. Top with the chives and kelp powder. Serve.

Note: To make your own nut/seed milk (recommended), blend ¾ cup nuts and/or seeds with 2 cups of filtered water. Blend well and strain. See page 35 for more information on nut/seed milks.

SPRING CONSOMMÉ WITH AVOCADO,
CHILI AND BABY DILL

Consomme: ♦

Serves 4-6

3 cups cucumber water (6 cucumbers)
2 cups vine ripen tomato water (8-9 tomatoes)[1]
2 teaspoons sea salt[2]
1 cup coconut water (or filtered water)
1 clove garlic
¼ teaspoon fresh chili, diced
2 tablespoons lemon juice
2 tablespoons flax oil
½ teaspoon cumin ground
garnish:
2 tablespoons mint, shredded fine
2 tablespoons dill feathers
½ cup avocado, diced (firm preferred)
¼ cup vine ripened tomato, diced small[3]
¼ cup tart apple, diced small

1. To release the natural water from the cucumber and tomatoes [place each in a separate bowl]:

   For the cucumbers: slice thinly and sprinkle one teaspoon of salt over the slices; massage the salt onto cucumbers until they begin to soften and release water.

   For the tomatoes: chop and sprinkle with one teaspoon of salt, massaging them until water is also released. Strain off liquid with a fine mesh strainer, save the water for the broth, and store the pulp for a future dish.

2. Blend the cucumber and tomato water with the coconut water, garlic, chili, lemon, flax oil and cumin in a high-speed blender. Pour again through a fine strainer to prevent foam.

3. Toss together, in a separate bowl, the avocado, apple, diced tomato and mint. Place a generous amount of mixture in each bowl.

4. Pour soup over and garnish with fresh dill. Serve chilled.

Kitchen Tip! The leftover tomato pulp is a great addition to any salad, blended with any tomato based sauce, or used blended with soaked flax seeds and spices for crackers.

How to "Hippocratize" this recipe:

[1] Substitute a combination of ¼ cup red bell pepper juice and ¾ cup celery juice for the tomato water.

[2] Substitute dulse, Bragg Liquid Aminos, Nama Shoyu, kelp or celery powder for the Celtic sea salt.

[3] Substitute ¼ cup of finely diced red bell pepper for the diced tomato.

Miso Soup with Arame, Shiitake and Spring Onion ◊

Serves 6

½ cup dark barley miso[1]
5 cups filtered water
3 cloves garlic
2 inch piece of ginger, chopped
2 small chiles, chopped
½ tablespoon toasted sesame oil[2]

1½ tablespoons tamari
pinch of sea salt[3]
¼ cup arame sea weed, dry
¼ cup fresh shiitake mushrooms, stemmed and sliced thin
3 tablespoons green onions, diced small

1. In high-speed blender, blend all except the arame, mushroom and green onion. Blend until smooth.

2. Pour through a fine mesh strainer and discard pulp.

3. Toss in the dried arame and shiitake slices. Serve warm and garnish with green onions.

How to "Hippocratize" this recipe:

[1] Substitute Bragg Liquid Aminos, to taste, for the miso.

[2] Substitute raw, unrefined sesame oil for the toasted sesame oil.

[3] Substitute dulse, Bragg Liquid Aminos, Nama Shoyu, kelp powder or celery powder for the Celtic sea salt.

Hippocrates' Green Soup

YIELD: 4 CUPS

1 - 1½ cups chopped fresh herbs
   of your choice
1 cup chopped cucumber
½ avocado
½ cup chopped celery

¼ cup chopped scallion
¾ teaspoon kelp powder
2 cups green juice*
1 teaspoon fresh lemon juice, optional

In a blender, combine all ingredients. Blend well and season to taste. Serve.

* See page 20 for Hippocrates' Green Juice recipe.

Kelly's Favorite Super Green Soup

YIELD: 2½ CUPS

2 cups chopped dark leafy greens
½ cup whole leaf dulse, snipped into pieces
¼ cup chopped scallion
¼ cup sauerkraut
1 cup water or green juice*

In a blender, combine all ingredients. Blend well and season to taste. Serve.

* See page 20 for Hippocrates' Green Juice recipe.

Borscht

YIELD: 5 CUPS

1 cup shredded green cabbage
½ cup finely diced red onion
2¾ cups chopped red beet
½ cup chopped red onion
½ avocado
1 stalk celery, roughly chopped

½ teaspoon fresh chopped thyme
2 cups water
1½ tablespoons fresh lemon juice, optional
1½ teaspoons Bragg Liquid Aminos
   or Nama Shoyu, optional

1. In a mixing bowl, combine cabbage and diced onion. Set aside.

2. In a blender, combine the remaining ingredients. Blend well and season to taste. Pour over the cabbage and onion mixture and mix well.

Spinach Mint Soup

YIELD: 2-4 SERVINGS

1 cup fresh cucumber juice
1 cup chopped spinach
⅓ cup chopped red onion
⅓ cup chopped red bell pepper
¼ cup chopped fresh mint

¼ avocado
1 clove garlic
2 cups water
2 tablespoons Bragg Liquid Aminos
    or Nama Shoyu

In a blender, combine all ingredients. Blend until smooth and season to taste. Serve.

Curried Lentil Soup

YIELD: 3 CUPS

1 cup sprouted lentils
¼ cup sliced scallions
¼ cup chopped fresh cilantro
1½ tablespoons dulse flakes

1. In a mixing bowl, combine the lentils, scallions, cilantro, and dulse flakes. Set aside.

2. In a blender, combine the sauce ingredients. Blend well and season to taste. Pour this sauce over the chopped vegetable mixture. Allow to stand for at least 30 minutes before serving.

Sauce:
1 cup sprouted lentils
¼ cup chopped scallion
¼ cup chopped carrot
¼ cup chopped celery
½ tablespoon chopped fresh ginger
1 clove garlic
1½ teaspoons curry powder
½ teaspoon kelp powder
1 cup water
¼ cup raw sesame oil
1 tablespoon fresh lemon juice, optional
2 teaspoons Bragg Liquid Aminos
    or Nama Shoyu
⅛ teaspoon liquid stevia extract

Melon Soup

YIELD: 2 SERVINGS

½ ripe melon of your choice, contents roughly chopped

In a blender, blend the chopped melon well. Add a little pure water if necessary to get the blending process started. Serve immediately. Add a touch of your favorite spice, such as cinnamon, cardamom, clove, mint or ginger for an added flavor boost.

Note: So perfect in its own right! An excellent way to break a fast.

Sprout Based Dishes

Chapter 6

Eat more sprouts!

OF ALL THE FOODS AVAILABLE IN THE LIVING FOODS PROGRAM, sprouts, which are the germinated seeds of plants, offer the highest level of nutrition. Most sprouts are truly a 'living food,' as they are still connected to their source of life—or life force—when they are consumed. Technically, a food transitions from 'living food' to a 'raw food' when it is separated from its life force—the source of life and growth. If you want more vitality, then eat food like sprouts that are still connected to their life source.

Foods that are connected to their life force, or that have just recently been harvested, are not only the freshest but are also the most nutritious and life-giving in that they are growing, alive foods available when you consume them. This is why, at Hippocrates, we teach the 'Living Foods' Program with sprouts as the obvious foundation. Not only do sprouts provide a vast supply of vitamins, minerals, naturally occurring hormones, oxygen, phytonutrients and enzymes, they provide 'life' itself.

Using sprouts in their natural sprouted form in salads, dressings and soups is a wonderful way to access their healing potential. Directions on soaking and sprouting are provided in the Basic Procedures Section on page 19. This section is for those of you who wish to integrate even more sprouts into your daily fare. Use it when you want to prepare fantastic and super-nutritious entrées!

Eat more sprouts!
Any sprouted bean or grain used in the recipes can be substituted for any other sprouted bean or grain. If the recipe calls for sprouted buckwheat and you want to use sprouted rye or sprouted lentils, feel free to do so.

Eat more sprouts!
You may wish to use just the main part of the recipe and skip the dressing for any of the following recipes. Dressings are not essential, but will affect taste, texture and firmness of other foods. Some people prefer to use just the chopped vegetable and sprout portion of the recipe and squeeze a little lemon, add some sea vegetables or sauerkraut on their food. It is up to you. Eliminating dressing will lighten up any salad.

So what can we do to have a more vital and vibrant life?
Eat more sprouts!

Mexicali Quinoa ⓓ

YIELD: 4 CUPS

3 cups sprouted quinoa
1 cup corn
½ cup finely diced red onion
½ cup thinly sliced scallion
½ cup finely diced red bell pepper
½ cup chopped fresh cilantro

Dressing:
1½ tablespoons chopped scallion
1 clove garlic
1 teaspoon kelp powder
1 pinch cayenne
½ cup extra virgin olive oil
3 tablespoons fresh lemon juice, optional

1. In a mixing bowl, combine the quinoa, corn, red onion, scallion, red bell pepper and cilantro.

2. In a blender, combine the dressing ingredients. Blend well and season to taste. Add the dressing to the mixing bowl and toss to combine.

Tip: 1 cup dry quinoa = 3 cups sprouted quinoa

Stuffed Zucchini ⓓ

YIELD: 8 HALVES

4 zucchini, halved
2 cups sprouted spelt
1 tablespoon dulse flakes
1 teaspoon poultry seasoning
1 teaspoon kelp powder
½ teaspoon garlic powder

3 tablespoons water
1 tablespoon extra virgin olive oil
½ cup finely diced carrot
½ cup finely diced celery
½ cup finely diced onion
½ cup chopped fresh parsley

1. Scoop out the middle of the zucchini so that it can be stuffed. Set prepared zucchini aside.

2. In a food processor, combine the sprouted spelt, dulse flakes, poultry seasoning, kelp powder, and garlic powder. Process to puree as much as possible. Add the water and olive oil and process further. The mixture will be lumpy and sticky.

3. By hand, mix in the carrot, celery, onion, and parsley. Season to taste. Stuff the zucchini. Dehydrate 4-6 hours or until desired level of "dryness" is achieved.

Marinated Sprouted Bean Salad

YIELD: 3 CUPS

2 cups sprouted beans
  (adzuki, garbanzo, mung, etc.)
¾ cup chopped fresh parsley
½ cup finely diced red onion

½ cup finely diced red bell pepper
¼ cup dulse flakes
¼ cup Hippocrates' House Dressing

In a mixing bowl, combine all ingredients. Mix well and season to taste. Allow to marinate at least 30 minutes before serving.

Buckwheat Tabouleh
YIELD: 5 CUPS

1½ cups sprouted hulled buckwheat,
   dehydrated for 3-5 hours
1½ cups chopped fresh parsley
1 cup finely chopped red bell pepper
¾ cup finely diced cucumber
½ cup finely diced red onion
¼ cup chopped fresh mint

Dressing:
1 clove garlic
2 teaspoons kelp powder
1 teaspoon ground cumin
1 pinch ground turmeric
½ cup extra virgin olive oil
3 - 4 tablespoons fresh lemon juice, optional
3 tablespoons water
2 - 3 drops liquid stevia extract

1. In a mixing bowl, combine the sprouted buckwheat, parsley, bell pepper, cucumber, onion and mint.

2. In a blender, combine the dressing ingredients. Add some fresh mint if desired. Blend well and season to taste.

3. Combine the dressing and salad mixture and mix well. Season to taste and serve.

Spelt Surprise ⓓ

YIELD: 7 CUPS

3 cups sprouted spelt
1 cup diced yellow squash
1 cup diced celery
1 cup quartered mushrooms
½ cup diced red bell pepper
½ cup diced onion
½ cup chopped fresh dill
½ cup chopped fresh parsley

Dressing:
½ cup Hippocrates' House Dressing
½ cup chopped red bell pepper
¼ cup fresh dill stems or leaves
¼ cup fresh parsley stems
1 scallion, chopped
½ tablespoon dried tarragon
1 teaspoon kelp powder
¼ teaspoon celery seed
¼ cup water

1. In a mixing bowl, combine the spelt, yellow squash, celery, mushrooms, diced bell pepper, diced onion, parsley and dill. Toss to combine and set aside.

2. In a blender, combine the house dressing, chopped red bell pepper, dill and parsley stems, scallion, tarragon, kelp powder, celery seed and water. Blend well and season to taste.

3. Combine the dressing and salad mixture, mix well, and season to taste.

Note: You may also make this salad without dressing, blend it with enough water to make a thick batter, and spread on a dehydrator tray to make a nice veggie-loaded cracker.

Cauliflower Garbanzo Italienne ⓓ

YIELD: 5 CUPS

2 cups chopped cauliflower
¾ cup sprouted garbanzo beans
½ cup diced red bell pepper
½ cup diced red onion
⅓ cup chopped fresh parsley

Dressing:
¼ cup sprouted garbanzo beans
1 clove garlic
½ tablespoon Frontier Pizza Seasoning
¼ cup extra virgin olive oil
¼ cup water
1 tablespoon fresh lemon juice, optional
½ teaspoon Bragg Liquid Aminos
   or Nama Shoyu
⅛ teaspoon liquid stevia extract

1. In a mixing bowl, combine the cauliflower, ¾ cup garbanzos, red bell pepper, onion and parsley.

2. In a blender, combine the dressing ingredients. Blend until smooth and creamy and season to taste.

3. Combine the dressing and salad mixture. Marinate at least 1 hour. Season to taste and serve.

Sprouted Raw Hummus

YIELD: 3 CUPS

2½ cups sprouted chick peas
1 cup chopped cucumber and/or cauliflower
1 cup chopped zucchini
2 - 3 cloves garlic
2 tablespoons ground cumin
1 tablespoon coriander seeds, ground
2 teaspoons kelp powder

⅓ cup water
3 tablespoons extra virgin olive oil
2½ tablespoons fresh lemon juice, optional
1 tablespoon Bragg Liquid Aminos
    or Nama Shoyu
¼ teaspoon liquid stevia extract, optional

1. In a food processor, combine all ingredients. Process until a smooth, thick dip is achieved.

Variations:
• Add any fresh herbs.
• Substitute more zucchini for some of the garbanzo beans to lighten.
• For another version use sprouted green peas instead of, or in combination with, chick peas.

Caraway Carrot Rye ⓓ

YIELD: 4½ CUPS

3 cups sprouted rye
3 cups shredded carrot
½ cup diced red onion
½ cup chopped fresh dill
1 teaspoon caraway seed

Dressing:
⅓ cup chopped red onion
¼ cup chopped fresh dill
1 clove garlic
1½ teaspoons kelp powder
1 teaspoon caraway seed
½ cup extra virgin olive oil
1½ tablespoons fresh lemon juice, optional
⅛ teaspoon liquid stevia extract

1. In a mixing bowl, combine the rye, carrot, ½ cup diced red onion, ½ cup chopped dill and 1 teaspoon caraway seed.

2. In a blender, combine the dressing ingredients. Blend well and season to taste.
   Combine the dressing and salad mixture. Let marinate for at least 30 minutes before serving.

Mushroom Kamut Pilaf

YIELD: 5½ CUPS

2 cups sprouted kamut
2 cups sliced crimini mushrooms
½ cup diced red onion
½ cup diced red bell pepper
½ cup chopped fresh parsley

Dressing:
½ cup chopped red bell pepper
⅛ cup chopped red onion
1 clove garlic
2 tablespoons dulse flakes
1 tablespoon paprika
½ teaspoon poultry seasoning
½ cup extra virgin olive oil
¼ cup water
1 tablespoon fresh lemon juice, optional
1 teaspoon Bragg Liquid Aminos
4 - 6 drops liquid stevia extract

1. In a mixing bowl, combine the kamut, mushrooms, red onion, bell pepper, and parsley.

2. In a blender, combine the dressing ingredients. Blend well and season to taste. Combine the dressing and salad mixture. Mix well; allow to marinate for at least 20 minutes before serving.

Cauliflower *with* Avocado *and* Olives

Avocado Based Dishes

CHAPTER 7

WHILE EVERY DAY IS A BLESSED DAY, it seems extra blessed on those days when avocados are served at Hippocrates. The avocado is a beautiful, sensual, satisfying food that we usually incorporate into our menus twice a week. From a frequency perspective, this is a good guideline for the average person to follow. Over-consuming 'good fats' can even have a detrimental effect. Avocados are widely available in most stores now. They come in many shapes and sizes, from the most commonly found Hass to our large and lovely Florida avocado. Avocados are ready when they give in slightly to applied pressure. The ripe ones that are slightly firm are best for salads that call for diced or sliced avocado. The very ripe, softer ones are great for dressings and dips such as guacamole. Avocado does oxidize and spoil rather quickly once its skin has been pierced, so it is best to consume most avocado-based dishes the same day. You may be able to stretch foods out to a second day, but fresher foods not only tastes better, they are better for you.

Coleslaw with Avo Mayo

YIELD: 5 CUPS

3 cups thinly sliced green cabbage
1 cup thinly sliced red cabbage
1 cup shredded carrot
1 cup thinly sliced celery
½ cup chopped fresh parsley

Dressing:
½ avocado
½ clove garlic
¼ teaspoon cayenne
¼ teaspoon kelp powder
¼ cup water
2 tablespoons fresh lemon juice, optional
½ - 1 teaspoon Bragg Liquid Aminos
   or Nama Shoyu
4 - 5 drops liquid stevia extract

1. In a mixing bowl, combine the cabbage, carrot, celery and parsley.

2. In a blender, combine the avocado, garlic, cayenne, kelp, water, lemon juice, Bragg Liquid Aminos or Nama Shoyu, and stevia. Blend well and season to taste.

3. Combine the dressing and salad mixture. Let stand at least 30 minutes before serving.

Cauliflower with Avocado and Olives

(photo at left)

YIELD: 3 CUPS

2 cups chopped cauliflower, small pieces
1 avocado, diced
¼ cup diced red onion
¼ cup chopped fresh basil

¼ cup Greek sun-dried olives,
   pitted and chopped
⅛ cup finely diced red bell pepper
2 tablespoons fresh lemon juice, optional

In a mixing bowl, combine all ingredients. Season to taste and serve.

Spinach Avocado Dip

YIELD: 2½ CUPS

3 cups spinach
2 cups avocado, chopped
1 clove garlic, pressed
1 tablespoon Frontier Pizza Seasoning
2 tablespoons fresh lemon juice, optional

½ tablespoon Bragg Liquid Aminos
  or Nama Shoyu
⅓ cup finely diced red bell pepper
⅓ cup finely diced red onion

1. In a food processor, finely chop the spinach.

2. Add to the food processor the avocado, garlic, pizza seasoning, lemon juice and Bragg Liquid Aminos or Nama Shoyu. Process to puree. Transfer this mixture to a mixing bowl.

3. Stir in the chopped bell pepper and onion, and mix well. Season to taste and serve.

Sprout Stuffed Avocado

YIELD: 2 HALVES

1 avocado, halved
¼ cup chopped onion sprouts
¼ cup chopped alfalfa sprouts
2 tablespoons minced celery
2 tablespoons shredded carrot

2 tablespoons chopped fresh parsley
1 tablespoon extra virgin olive oil
1 clove garlic, pressed
Bragg Liquid Aminos, dulse,
  or kelp granules to taste

1. In a bowl, combine all ingredients except the avocado. Mix well and season to taste.

2. Stuff each avocado half with the mixture and serve.

Avocado Rainbowl

YIELD: 3½ CUPS

1-2 large avocados, diced
½ cup diced red cabbage
½ cup chopped snow peas
½ cup shredded carrot
½ cup diced red bell pepper
⅓ cup shredded golden beet

¼ cup chopped fresh basil
2 tablespoons diced red onion
1 teaspoon fresh lemon juice
Bragg Liquid Aminos, dulse,
  or kelp granules to taste, optional

Mix all ingredients together in a bowl and season to taste. Serve.

Stuffed Avocados

YIELD: 6 HALVES

1 cup finely diced cucumber
3 tablespoons finely diced red bell pepper
2 tablespoons finely diced red onion

½ teaspoon dulse flakes
¼ teaspoon kelp & cayenne
3 avocados, halved

1. In a bowl, combine all ingredients except the avocado. Mix well and season to taste.

2. Stuff the vegetable mixture into each avocado half and serve.

Kale Avocado Salad ⋏

Serves 2–4

1 head of kale, shredded or finely chopped
2 ounces tomato, diced[1]
½ avocado, chopped
2 tablespoons flax oil

1½ teaspoons lemon juice
2 tablespoons red onion or leek, diced
½ teaspoon sea salt[2]

Toss all ingredients together in mixing bowl, squeezing as you mix to 'wilt' the kale and cream the avocado. Serve immediately.

Variation:
· Add chopped fresh herbs or your choice of diced vegetable.
· This dish is also great when chard or spinach is substituted for the kale.

How to "Hippocratize" this recipe:

[1] Substitute diced red bell pepper for the tomato.

[2] Substitute dulse, Bragg Liquid Aminos, Nama Shoyu, kelp powder or celery powder for the Celtic sea salt.

Guacamole

YIELD: 4 CUPS

3 cups mashed avocado
½ cup finely diced red onion
½ cup finely diced red bell pepper
½ cup shredded carrot
½ cup chopped fresh cilantro
1 - 2 cloves garlic, pressed

1 teaspoon ground cumin
cayenne to taste
2 tablespoons fresh lemon juice
Bragg Liquid Aminos, dulse
   or kelp granules to taste

In a bowl, combine all ingredients. By hand, mash the ingredients together, mixing well. Season to taste and serve.

Creamy Peas and Peppers

YIELD: 3 CUPS

1½ cups fresh peas or chopped snow peas*
1 cup large diced red bell pepper
½ cup whole leaf dulse, snipped
½ avocado, diced
¼ cup diced red onion
1 tablespoon dried tarragon, or
2 tablespoons chopped fresh tarragon

Dressing:
½ avocado
½ clove garlic
⅛ teaspoon cayenne
¼ cup water
1 teaspoon fresh lemon juice, optional
2 drops liquid stevia extract

1. In a mixing bowl, combine the peas, bell pepper, dulse, ½ avocado, onion and tarragon.

2. In a blender, combine the other ½ avocado, garlic, cayenne, water, lemon juice and stevia. Blend well and season to taste.

3. Combine the vegetable and dressing mixtures. Season to taste and serve.

* Sliced or diced celery may be substituted for the peas.

Awakening Avocados

YIELD: 4 HALVES

2 avocados, halved
½ cup shredded beet
¼ cup shredded horseradish
¼ cup shredded carrot

¼ cup chopped fresh parsley
1 teaspoon fresh lemon juice
Bragg Liquid Aminos, dulse,
    or kelp granules to taste, optional

In a mixing bowl, combine all ingredients except the avocado. Mix well and season to taste. Stuff this mixture in each avocado half and serve.

Nut and Seed Based Dishes

CHAPTER 8

NUTS AND SEEDS are wonderful in so many ways. Not only are they powerhouses of stored nutrients and energy, but they also allow us to expand our Living Foods Diet by providing a wonderful complement to fresh raw vegetable and sprout salads. In addition, they provide that "crunch factor" that so many of us crave. Using nuts and seeds, we can make everything from entrées, such as burgers, patés and loafs, to creamy sauces, pie crusts, cookies and cakes. Nuts and seeds help us create a variety of raw and healthy versions of familiar dishes that many people enjoy.

Nuts and seeds (especially sunflower, pine nut, pumpkin, hemp, hazelnut, and sesame) fall into the protein category with regard to food combining, as do all of the recipes in this section. Therefore it is best to combine these proteins with foods that are complementary, such as fresh green sprout salads. See the Food Combining section on pages 15-17 for more information.

Also remember to soak all nuts and seeds before using them. This will release their natural enzyme inhibitors and increase nutrition and digestibility. Soak overnight or all day. As long as you soak for an 8-10 hour time span, you have initiated germination. Once soaked, nuts and seeds must either be used or dehydrated to last indefinitely, depending on the freshness of the nut/seed. Refrigerated nuts and seeds may last up to a week. Set up your 'Living Foods' kitchen by purchasing a variety of your favorite nuts and seeds, then soak, dehydrate and store them in airtight containers. You will have delightful, ready-to-eat snacks, and convenient, ready-to-use foods for preparing other dishes. Preparing in advance eliminates the need to plan ahead of time to make any dish that requires soaked and dehydrated nuts and seeds. If a recipe calls for nuts that are only soaked and you've already dehydrated them, you can simply rehydrate them by placing them in pure water for a minimum of 20 minutes. They will quickly absorb the water and soften, making them easier to process.

Nuts and seeds require more energy for digestion. They are also one of the easiest foods to overeat; keep moderation in mind. At Hippocrates we use nuts and seeds in our preparations only twice a week, as with avocados. This is an excellent guideline for the average person.

Cannelloni Bites with Almond Herb Ricotta and Tomato Compote

Cannelloni

Makes 10 small plates

3 zucchini, sliced thin lengthwise
   with mandolin
2 cup almonds, soaked 10-12 hours
1 cup pine nuts
2 tablespoons olive oil
2 tablespoons lemon juice
½ teaspoon sea salt[1]

1 tablespoon garlic
½ teaspoon black pepper[2]
3 tablespoons water
¼ cup fresh olives, minced
1 tablespoon sage or oregano, minced
2 tablespoons basil, fresh and minced
Tomato relish (see recipe below)[3]

1. In a food processor, blend the almonds, pine nuts, olive oil, lemon juice, salt, garlic and water until it becomes a smooth, thick paste – this basic part of the recipe should taste balanced. If not, then emphasize the base components of salt, fat or acid that are needed.

2. Hand-mix in the olives and herbs.

To assemble:

1. Using a mandolin, slice the zucchini lengthwise in paper-thin slices to get long thin strips.

2. Place 2 strips side-by-side, slightly overlapping, to create a wider strip.

3. With one of the ends facing you, place a tablespoon scoop of pate near the end of the strip closest to you.

4. Fold over zucchini and then proceed to gently roll until a cylinder is formed with the paste holding the round together; this creates a cannelloni shape.

5. Place on screen of dehydrator sheet and dehydrate for 2-3 hours or until firm. Serve with tomato relish.

How to "Hippocratize" this recipe:

[1] Substitute dulse, Bragg Liquid Aminos, Nama Shoyu, kelp powder or celery powder for the Celtic sea salt.

[2] Substitute cayenne pepper for black pepper, or omit pepper entirely.

[3] Instead of serving with tomato relish, serve with Raw Red Pepper Marinara (see recipe on page 53).

Tomato Relish

½ cup sun-dried tomatoes,
   soaked 1-3 hours until softened
2 large tomatoes, chopped
2 cloves garlic, finely minced

2 tablespoons basil, chiffonade
2 tablespoons olive oil
¼ teaspoon Celtic salt
1 teaspoon white pepper

Hand mix all ingredients well. Do not keep for more than two days. Serve with cannelloni.

Kitchen Tip! For faster production, lay 12-15 zucchini strips down at a time. Move down the line and place paté on each first, and then roll each zucchini. Working with a production line makes preparation time go by in a flash.

Wild Mushroom Quiche Ⓓ

YIELD: 1 QUICHE

Crust:
3 cups walnuts, soaked
¼ cup flax seeds, ground
1 clove garlic, pressed
½ teaspoon dried thyme or Herbs De Provence
½ teaspoon dried tarragon
½ tablespoon Bragg Liquid Aminos
Filling:
Marinate 3½ cups sliced crimini mushrooms
¾ cup sliced scallions
⅓ cup extra virgin olive oil
½ tablespoon Bragg Liquid Aminos

Blend
1 cup raw sesame tahini OR soaked walnuts
1½ teaspoons psyllium husks powder
1 pinch ground nutmeg
1 cup water
3 tablespoons fresh lemon juice, optional
1½ tablespoons Bragg Liquid Aminos
5 drops liquid stevia extract

1. In a food processor, combine all crust ingredients. Process until a dough is formed and the walnuts are very well chopped. Season to taste.

2. Press the crust mixture into the plate and dehydrate overnight.

3. Marinate the scallions and mushrooms in ⅓ cup olive oil and ½ tablespoon Bragg Liquid Aminos for at least 1 hour.

4. In a blender, combine the tahini or walnuts, psyllium, nutmeg, water, lemon juice, Bragg Liquid Aminos and stevia. Blend well until smooth and creamy. Fold this mixture into the marinated mushrooms and green onions. Spread evenly over the crust. Chill at least 1 hour and serve. The psyllium will thicken with time.

Hearty Pasta with Peppers, Mushrooms and "Meat" Sauce

YIELD: 4½ CUPS

2 cups Vegetable Spiraghetti, see page 94
1½ cups sliced crimini mushrooms
1 cup julienne bell pepper
¼ cup chiffonade fresh basil
1 cup Raw Red Pepper Marinara, see page 53

Optional Nut "Meat":
1½ cups walnuts, soaked & dehydrated
½ teaspoon Italian seasoning
¼ teaspoon garlic powder
½ teaspoon Bragg Liquid Aminos
   or Nama Shoyu

1. In a mixing bowl, combine the vegetable spiraghetti, mushrooms, peppers and basil.

2. Add the red pepper marinara sauce to the mixing bowl.

3. To make the nut "meat" for a "meaty" sauce: In a food processor, process the walnuts, Italian seasoning and garlic powder to a fine crumble. Add the Bragg Liquid Aminos or Nama Shoyu and process again. Add this to the mixing bowl with the pasta mixture and sauce. Toss all. Allow to marinate for at least 30 minutes before serving.

Pumpkin Seed Hummus

YIELD: 3½ CUPS

2 cups pumpkin seeds, soaked
1 cup chopped cucumber, optional
1 cup chopped zucchini, optional
2 cloves garlic
2 tablespoons ground cumin
1 tablespoon ground coriander seed
2 teaspoons kelp powder

¾ cup water
2½ tablespoons fresh lemon juice, optional
2 tablespoons pumpkin seed oil
1 tablespoon Bragg Liquid Aminos
   or Nama Shoyu
¼ teaspoon liquid stevia extract, optional

In a strong blender, combine all ingredients. Blend well until very smooth. You will need to use a spatula or blender plunger to keep the mixture moving in the blender. Season to taste and serve.

Optional Add-ins:
¼ teaspoon cayenne pepper, ½ cup chopped scallion, 1 cup chopped fresh herbs of your choice

Alternate Version: Sunny Hummus
• Substitute 2 cups sunflower seeds, soaked, for the pumpkin seeds.
• Substitute 2 tablespoons raw sesame tahini for the pumpkin seed oil.

Kale, Broccoli and Pumpkin Seeds

YIELD: 3½ CUPS

2 cups chiffonade lacinato kale
1½ cups small broccoli florettes
⅓ cup finely diced red onion
⅓ cup pumpkin seeds, soaked & dehydrated

1. In a bowl, combine the kale, broccoli, onion and ⅓ cup pumpkin seeds.

2. In a blender, combine the remaining ingredients. Blend well and season to taste. Toss the dressing and the salad mixture. Allow to marinate for at least 30 minutes before serving.

Dressing:
½ cup pumpkin seeds, soaked & dehydrated
1 clove garlic
½ teaspoon ground cumin
1 pinch cayenne
¼ cup water
2 tablespoons raw pumpkin seed oil
2 tablespoons fresh lemon juice, optional
1 teaspoon Bragg Liquid Aminos

Stuffed Mushrooms ⓓ

YIELD: 2 MUSHROOMS

2 portobello mushroom caps
1 cup chopped red bell pepper
¾ cup walnuts, soaked & dehydrated
½ cup chopped carrot
½ cup chopped red onion

⅓ cup chopped fresh basil
10 sun-dried black olives, pitted
1 clove garlic
1 teaspoon dried oregano

1. Clean and set aside the portobello caps, gill side up.

2. In a food processor, combine the remaining ingredients and process to form a paté consistency. Season to taste. Use this mixture to fill the tops of the mushrooms. Let stand 30 minutes. Cut in pieces and serve, or leave whole and dehydrate overnight, then serve.

Note: Any of your favorite paté or nut loaf recipes can be used to stuff mushrooms, celery, cucumbers, lettuce leaves, squash, peppers or any other suitable vegetables.

Nutmeat Loaf ⓓ

YIELD: 1 LOAF

3 cups pecans, soaked
3 cups walnuts, soaked
2 red bell peppers, chopped
1 cup chopped carrot
2 tablespoons paprika

1 tablespoon garlic powder
1 tablespoon poultry seasoning
Bragg Liquid Aminos or Nama Shoyu to taste
1 cup onion, finely diced
1 cup celery, finely diced

1. In a mixing bowl, combine all ingredients except the onion and celery. Mix well. Process this mixture through an appropriate juicer using the blank (homogenizing) attachment. Season to taste.

2. By hand, mix in the onion and celery. Form into a loaf shape on a dehydrator tray; use a teflex sheet or unbleached parchment paper beneath. Dehydrate overnight. Top with Red Pepper Ketchup (page 53) several hours before serving and return to the dehydrator for 2-3 more hours. Slice and serve.

Creamed Spinach

YIELD: 2½ CUPS

3 cups spinach
½ cup julienne onion

1. In a mixing bowl, combine the spinach and onion.

2. In a blender, combine the remaining ingredients. Blend well and season to taste.

3. Combine the spinach and dressing. Mix well. Enjoy just as it is or dehydrate for a few hours to wilt and warm the spinach.

Dressing:
½ cup pine nuts, soaked
1 clove garlic
¾ teaspoon kelp powder
⅛ teaspoon ground nutmeg
½ cup water
1 tablespoon fresh lemon juice, optional
⅛ teaspoon liquid stevia extract

Sunflower Almond Paté

YIELD: 3½ CUPS

1 cup sunflower seeds, soaked
1 cup almonds, soaked
1½ stalks celery, chopped
⅔ cup chopped red bell pepper
⅔ cup chopped broccoli stems
1 clove garlic

1 tablespoon paprika
1 teaspoon onion powder
1 tablespoon Bragg Liquid Aminos
    or Nama Shoyu
½ cup chopped fresh parsley

1. In a mixing bowl, combine all ingredients except the parsley. Toss to combine.
    Using the blank (homogenizing) attachment of an appropriate juicer, process the mixture.

2. By hand, mix in the parsley. Season to taste and serve.

Note: This paté can be dehydrated to make crackers or used to stuff vegetables.

Walnut Tacos

YIELD: 2 CUPS

3 cups walnuts, soaked & dehydrated
1 clove garlic
2 tablespoons chili powder

¼ teaspoon cayenne
1 teaspoon Bragg Liquid Aminos

In a food processor, combine all ingredients. Process, pulsing, until desired texture is achieved. Season to taste.

To Make a Taco:
Use a romaine lettuce leaf (for a "hard shell" taco) or a collard green (for a "soft shell" taco). Add some taco stuffing "meat" and toppings (shredded carrot, scallion, chopped onion, hot sauce, shredded lettuce, etc.) Fold or roll and serve.

Brazil Nut Loaf ⬣

YIELD: 4 CUPS

2 cups Brazil nuts, soaked in water
2 cups roughly chopped carrot
¼ cup chopped red onion
2 stalks celery, roughly chopped
1 clove garlic
1½ teaspoons caraway seed
1 teaspoon fennel seed
1 teaspoon onion powder

Optional Stir-ins:
2 teaspoons Bragg Liquid Aminos
    or Nama Shoyu
½ cup chopped fresh parsley and/or dill
¼ cup finely diced onion
¼ cup finely diced celery

In a bowl, combine all ingredients except stir-ins. Process this mixture through an appropriate juicer using the homogenizing attachment. Season to taste. Add the optional stir-ins if desired.

Note: This paté can be dehydrated to make crackers or burger patties.

Roasted Tomato[1] stuffed with Pignoli Spinach Paté and Young Dill ⟩

Pignoli Spinach Paté:
Makes 4 cups or stuffs 8-10 tomatoes

1½ cup pine nuts
2 cloves garlic
2 tablespoons lemon juice
⅓ cup water
1 teaspoon nutmeg
½ teaspoon Celtic sea salt[2]
2 tablespoons olive oil

1½ cups red bell pepper, diced
1 cup sun dried black olives, pitted and minced
2 tablespoons basil, fresh and minced
3 tablespoons dill, fresh and minced
1½ tablespoons oregano, fresh and minced
1½ cup baby spinach, shredded

1. Clean and slice ¼ off tops of tomatoes, hollowing out slightly.

2. In a food processor, process the following until smooth: pine nuts, garlic, lemon, water, nutmeg, salt, and olive oil.

3. Hand-mix remaining ingredients in a mixing bowl. Stuff tomatoes. Dehydrate for 1-2 hours before serving.

Note: Can also be served as a dip with crudités.

How to "Hippocratize" this recipe:

[1] Instead of stuffing tomatoes, stuff red bell peppers, celery, cucumbers, zucchini or mushrooms.

[2] Substitute dulse, Bragg Liquid Aminos, Nama Shoyu, kelp powder or celery powder for the Celtic sea salt.

Sweet Potato Leek Latkes ⚑ Ⓓ

Serves 4

1½ cups sweet potatoes, peeled and chopped
1½ cups cauliflower, chopped
1 cup pine nuts
¼ cup leek, chopped
2 tablespoons onion powder

3 tablespoons flax oil
¼ cup filtered water
½ tablespoon Celtic sea salt[1]
2 tablespoons dried parsley

1. In food processor combine all ingredients and blend until the consistency is very smooth.

2. Pour mixture in a high-speed blender and blend until completely smooth. Adjust salt.

3. Pour mixture to form a ¼ inch thick burger-size patties on a dehydrator sheet lined with teflex,.

4. Dehydrate at 105 degrees for 6 hours. Flip latkes off teflex directly onto the screen.
   Continue to dehydrate 6-8 hours, or until optimum dryness is achieved.
   Serve with Apple Relish[2] and Cashew Sour Cream[3].

Apple Relish[2]
Makes 2 cups: 3 tablespoons equal one serving

1 cup dried apples, rehydrated
1 cup apples, diced in small pieces
2 tablespoons flax oil
1½ tablespoons lemon juice
1 tablespoon onion powder

2 tablespoons red onion, minced
2 tablespoons parsley, chopped
½ tablespoon cinnamon
1 teaspoon sea salt

1. In food processor, process the rehydrated apples until smooth. Add to a mixing bowl.

2. Hand-mix remaining ingredients into apple puree until thoroughly combined.

3. Serve with Latkes and Cashew Sour Cream.

Cashew Sour Cream[3]
Makes 1½ cups

2 cups cashews soaked 10-12 hours
2 tablespoons olive oil
3 tablespoons apple cider vinegar
1 tablespoon agave
½ teaspoon Celtic sea salt

Blend all ingredients in a high-speed blender until smooth.

How to "Hippocratize" this recipe:

[1] Substitute dulse, Bragg Liquid Aminos, Nama Shoyu, kelp powder or celery powder for the Celtic sea salt.

[2] Omit the Apple Relish: Top with marinated sweet onions if topping is desired (see recipe below).

[3] Instead of Cashew Sour Cream, use the Avo Mayo (see recipe on page 52).

Chive Oil
Makes 1 cup

2 cup chives, loosely packed
½ cup parsley, loosely packed
1 cup neutral oil
½ teaspoon Celtic sea salt[1]
Freshly cracked black pepper to taste[2]

1. Blend all ingredients in a blender until a smooth consistency is achieved.
   Note: you may need to fold with rubber spatula while blending to keep the mixture moving.

2. Pour mixture through a fine-mesh strainer, stirring constantly so that all oil is separated. Discard or save the pulp for future use. Garnish dishes and soups with a drizzle. Will keep up to a week in the fridge.

How to "Hippocratize" this recipe:

[1] Substitute dulse, Bragg Liquid Aminos, Nama Shoyu, kelp powder or celery powder for the Celtic sea salt.

[2] Substitute cayenne pepper for black pepper, or omit pepper entirely.

Marinated Onions Ⓓ
Yield: approximately 1 cup

1 red or yellow onion, julienne cut or sliced
Bragg Liquid Aminos, Nama Shoyu, or other flavor enhancer

Method of Preparation: Toss the chopped onions with just enough Bragg Liquid Aminos, Nama Shoyu, or other flavor enhancer to barely coat. Marinate for a minimum of 30 minutes. Drain and rinse them off or use as is. Dehydrate them for a crunchy treat on salads and other dishes.

Vegetable and Seaweed Based Dishes

CHAPTER 9

THERE IS SUCH AN ABUNDANCE OF FOOD when it comes to vegetables. Colors, flavors, textures, nutrients, antioxidants, phytochemicals and pleasures abound! The dishes in this section are free from any other concentrated foods, such as sprouted grains, beans, avocados or nuts, so they can combine with anything except fruit. You may eliminate the dressing in any recipe for a lighter salad.

Sea vegetables are an incredible group of foods that many people have not even begun to explore. Aside from providing hearty tastes and textures, sea vegetables provide an abundance of trace minerals and help pull heavy metal contaminants from the body. Sea vegetables (sometimes called seaweed) can be added to any salad and most recipes. If you dislike the taste of sea vegetables on their own, consider using small amounts in all of your recipes. Most sea vegetables do not alter taste or flavor of recipes when added in small amounts. Using them this way, you receive all of the benefits while enjoying the tastes you prefer.

You will find sea vegetables in most health food stores and many Asian supermarkets. There are also excellent companies who harvest and sell seaweed in bulk. Check the Resources section on page 141.

Cabbage and Peas Tarragon *(photo at left)*

YIELD: 4½ CUPS

2 cups fresh peas
2 cups small diced green and/or red cabbage
½ cup chopped fresh parsley
⅓ cup diced red onion
1 tablespoon dried tarragon

Dressing:
½ cup Hippocrates House Dressing,
  see page 22
¼ cup water

1. In a mixing bowl, combine the peas, cabbage, parsley, onion and 1 tablespoon tarragon. Set aside.

2. In a blender, combine the remaining ingredients. Blend well and season to taste.

3. Combine the dressing and salad mixture. Allow to marinate at least 30 minutes before serving.

Cauliflower with Dulse and Arugula

YIELD: 3 CUPS

3 cups chopped cauliflower
2 cups chopped arugula
½ cup finely diced red bell pepper
20 Greek sun-dried olives, pitted & chopped
1 clove garlic, pressed

1 tablespoon dulse flakes
1 teaspoon dried oregano
1½ tablespoons extra virgin olive oil
1 teaspoon fresh lemon juice, optional

1. In a food processor, pulse the cauliflower until finely chopped. Set aside in a mixing bowl.

2. Again in the food processor, finely chop the arugula. Add to the bowl with the cauliflower.

3. Add the remaining ingredients to the mixing bowl and toss. Season to taste and serve.

Vegetable Curry

YIELD: 5 CUPS

1 cup large diced red bell pepper
1 cup quartered mushrooms
1 cup small broccoli florets
1 cup small cauliflower florets
1 cup halved & sliced zucchini
½ cup chopped fresh cilantro, optional
⅓ cup halved & sliced carrot
2 scallions, sliced diagonally

Dressing:
½ cup Hippocrates' House Dressing,
   see page 22
½ cup chopped bell pepper
¼ cup chopped scallion
1 teaspoon curry powder
¼ cup water
1 tablespoon raw sesame oil
⅛ teaspoon liquid stevia extract

1. In a mixing bowl, combine the bell pepper, mushrooms, broccoli, cauliflower, zucchini, cilantro (optional), carrot and sliced scallions. Toss and set aside.

2. In a blender, combine the dressing ingredients. Blend well and season to taste.

3. Combine the vegetable mixture and dressing, and season to taste. Allow to stand for at least 30 minutes before serving.

Pasta Putanesca with Courgette, Fresh Olives and Cured Tomatoes ⟩

Pasta:

2 zucchini, sliced lengthwise with a mandolin and cut into thin linguine-size strips
9-10 leaves basil, fresh stacked and chiffonade
2 tablespoons thyme, minced
1 red bell pepper, sliced in paper-thin rounds
1 yellow bell pepper, sliced similarly

Sauce:

¼ cup olives: Kalamata, green and black, pitted and mixed
3 tablespoons capers, rinsed
½ cup sun-dried tomatoes, rehydrated and julienned[1]
3 tablespoons olive oil
1 tablespoon truffle oil (optional)
2 tablespoons lemon zest
2 cloves garlic, minced
2 small shallots or red onion, finely diced
1 fresh chile, minced (optional)
Celtic sea salt and freshly cracked black pepper to taste[2,3]

Garnish:

½ cup macadamia nuts, finely ground
½ tablespoon sea salt
½ tablespoon onion powder

1. For Pasta: In mixing bowl, toss the zucchini noodles, bell peppers, thyme and basil; set aside.

2. For Sauce: Coarsely chop the olives, capers and sun-dried tomato; place in a separate bowl. Toss with remaining sauce ingredients and stir thoroughly.

3. Prior to serving, toss the olive mix with the noodles. Salt to taste. For individual servings use 1 cup of pasta with ¼ cup of sauce; garnish each separately.

Garnish Prep:

1. Finely grind the unsoaked macadamia nuts into a fine meal with sea salt and onion powder.

2. Sprinkle on pasta prior to serving.

NOTE: Be sure when using a water-dense vegetable (as the pasta does) that you toss it with sauce just before serving. This will ensure that the natural water within the zucchini, in this case, is not released.

How to "Hippocratize" this recipe:

[1] For sauce, substitute ½ cup small diced red bell pepper for the sun-dried tomatoes.

[2] Use dulse, Bragg Liquid Aminos, Nama Shoyu, kelp powder or celery powder in place of the Celtic sea salt.

[3] Instead of black pepper, use either cayenne or omit pepper.

Vegetable Spiraghetti (Raw Pasta)

YIELD: 4½ CUPS

2 cups any root vegetable or squash
1 cup Raw Red Pepper Marinara, see page 53

Trim the ends off of whatever vegetable you are using. Using a turning vegetable slicer, such as the Saladacco or Benriner Turning Vegetable Slicer,* spiralize the root vegetable/squash. Top with your favorite sauce or dressing such as Raw Red Pepper Marinara (page 53), Macadamia Alfredo (page 57) and Pesto Dressing (page 52). Add chopped veggies and herbs if desired.

Vegetables that work well: turnip, beet, rutabaga, zucchini, yellow squash, black radish, butternut squash, daikon, parsnip, sweet potato and celery root.

* Highly recommended. See Resources, page 141.

Spanish Cabbage

YIELD: 5 CUPS

4 cups chopped green cabbage
½ cup finely diced red onion
¼ cup finely diced red bell pepper
2 scallions, thinly sliced

Dressing:
1 clove garlic
½ teaspoon kelp powder
1 pinch saffron
2 tablespoons extra virgin olive oil
1 tablespoon water
1 teaspoon fresh lemon juice, optional

1. In a food processor, pulse the cabbage until finely chopped. Set aside in a mixing bowl.

2. Add to the mixing bowl the red onion, bell pepper and scallion, and toss to mix.

3. In a blender, combine the remaining ingredients. Blend well and season to taste.

4. Combine the dressing and salad mixture. Mix well and season to taste. Serve.

Squash Ratatouille ⓓ

YIELD: 4½ CUPS

2 cups large diced zucchini
1 cup large diced yellow squash
1 cup large diced red bell pepper
1 cup sliced celery
¼ cup large diced red onion
¼ cup snipped dulse leaf, optional
¼ cup chopped fresh parsley
12 Greek sun-dried olives, pitted & chopped

Dressing:
1 cup chopped red bell pepper
1 clove garlic
1 teaspoon paprika
1 teaspoon Italian seasoning
1 teaspoon kelp powder
¼ cup water
2 tablespoons extra virgin olive oil
1 teaspoon fresh lemon juice, optional
6 drops liquid stevia extract

1. In a mixing bowl, combine the zucchini, yellow squash, red bell pepper, celery, onion, dulse (optional), parsley and olives.

2. In a blender, combine the dressing ingredients. Blend well and season to taste.

3. Combine the dressing and vegetable mixture. Mix well and season to taste. Allow to marinate at least 30 minutes before serving.

Beet Onion Salad ⓓ

YIELD: 5 CUPS

3 cups waffle sliced* red beet
1½ cups julienne red onion
½ cup chopped fresh parsley

Dressing:
⅓ cup extra virgin olive oil
⅛ cup fresh lemon juice, optional
½ teaspoon kelp powder
3 drops liquid stevia extract

1. In a mixing bowl, combine the beet, onion and parsley.

2. In a blender, combine the remaining ingredients. Blend well and season to taste.

3. Toss the dressing and vegetable mixture. Allow to marinate for at least 20 minutes before serving.

* Waffle slices are achieved using a mandolin. See product manual for instructions.

Lacinato Kale Ribbons

YIELD: 6 CUPS

5 cups chiffonade lacinato kale
1½ cups sliced celery
1 cup Greek sun-dried olives, pitted & chopped

1 cup whole leaf dulse, snipped into pieces
½ cup Hippocrates' House Dressing,
see page 22

In a mixing bowl, combine all ingredients. Mix well and season to taste.

Sea Lettuce Salad ⓓ

YIELD: 3 CUPS

3 cups dry sea lettuce, snipped into pieces
1 cup halved & sliced cucumber
1 cup sliced celery
½ cup fresh chopped cilantro
¼ cup sliced scallions

1 clove garlic, pressed
2 tablespoons raw sesame oil
2 teaspoons fresh lemon juice, optional
⅛ teaspoon cayenne

In a mixing bowl, combine all ingredients. Season to taste and serve.

Sesame Julienne ⓓ

YIELD: 4½ CUPS

1 cup julienne carrots
1 cup julienne celery
1 cup julienne red bell peppers
1 cup julienne zucchini
1 cup sliced shiitake mushrooms
2 scallions, sliced diagonally

2 tablespoons raw sesame oil
1 teaspoon fresh lemon juice, optional
1 teaspoon Bragg Liquid Aminos
**   or Nama Shoyu**
2 tablespoons sesame seeds, soaked &
**   dehydrated, optional**

In a mixing bowl, combine all ingredients and season to taste. Serve.

Shaved Fennel and Mandarin Salad with Wild Fennel Pollen ⟩

Serves 2-4

2 cups fennel, julienne thin
1 cup mandarin segments[1]
1 tablespoon lemon zest
2 tablespoons lemon juice
2½ tablespoons olive oil
1½ tablespoons lemon thyme, fresh and minced

1 tablespoon red jalapeno, seeded and
  minced (optional)
1 teaspoon Celtic salt[2]
½ teaspoon fennel pollen (optional)
Freshly cracked black pepper to taste[3]

1. Using a mandolin, carefully shave the fennel bulb.

2. In a medium mixing bowl, toss all ingredients well. Serve chilled.

Variation:
• Omit the mandarins and add shaved apples.

How to "Hippocratize" this recipe:

[1] Omit the mandarin oranges; use 1 tablespoon of orange zest and add 1 cup of yellow and/or orange bell peppers cut julienne style.

[2] Substitute dulse, Bragg Liquid Aminos, Nama Shoyu, kelp powder or celery powder for the Celtic sea salt.

[3] Substitute cayenne pepper for black pepper, or omit pepper entirely.

Dulse Italiano ⓓ

YIELD: 5 CUPS

2 cups whole leaf dulse, cut into bite-sized pieces
1 cup waffle* sliced yellow squash
1 cup waffle sliced zucchini
1 cup waffle sliced carrot
½ cup large diced red bell pepper

½ cup large diced orange bell pepper
¼ cup large diced red onion
½ cup chopped fresh basil and/or parsley
1 cup Red Pepper Italian Dressing, see page 55

In a bowl, combine all ingredients and mix well. Season to taste and serve. For best results, allow to marinate for at least 20 minutes before serving.

* Waffle slices are achieved using a mandolin. See product manual for instructions.

Sea Vegetable Salad ⓓ

YIELD: 3½ CUPS

½ ounce soaked Sea Veg Salad mix, or
½ ounce mixed dried sea-veggies,
  soaked in water for 10 minutes and drained
½ cup thinly sliced carrot

½ cup thinly sliced daikon radish
½ cup thinly sliced cucumber
2 scallions, sliced diagonally
½ cup Sesame Ginger Dressing, see page 53

In a mixing bowl, combine all ingredients. Toss well and allow to marinate for at least 10 minutes for a softer salad. For another variation of this salad, shred the carrot and daikon instead of slicing.

Optional Add-ins:
1 avocado, diced, ¼ cup chopped cilantro

"Seafood" Salad Ⓓ

YIELD: 4 CUPS

1 package soaked sea vegetable salad mix, or
1 cup mixed dry sea vegetables soaked in water
1 cup thinly sliced celery
1 cup shredded carrot
½ cup chopped fresh parsley
½ cup snipped dulse leaf
¼ cup diced onion

Dressing:
½ cup pine nuts, soaked in water
½ clove garlic
½ teaspoon kelp powder
½ teaspoon ground mustard seed
¼ teaspoon ground turmeric
⅛ teaspoon cayenne
⅓ - ½ cup water
1 teaspoon fresh lemon juice, optional
½ teaspoon Bragg Liquid Aminos
    or Nama Shoyu
4 drops liquid stevia extract

1. In a mixing bowl, combine the hydrated sea vegetables, celery, carrot, parsley, dulse and onion.

2. In a blender, combine the dressing ingredients. Blend well and season to taste.

3. Combine the dressing and salad mixture. Let stand at least 30 minutes before serving.

Sweet -N- Spicy Arame

YIELD: 2 CUPS

1 cup shredded carrot
1 cup arame or hijiki, hydrated
⅓ cup thinly sliced scallion

Dressing:
1 clove garlic
¾ teaspoon cayenne
¼ cup raw sesame oil
2 teaspoons fresh lemon juice, optional
⅛ teaspoon liquid stevia extract
½ teaspoon Bragg Liquid Aminos
    or Nama Shoyu

1. In a bowl, combine the carrot, arame and scallion.

2. In a blender, combine the dressing ingredients. Blend well and season to taste.

3. Combine the dressing and salad mixture. Season to taste and serve.

Desserts

CHAPTER 10

CONVENTIONAL DESSERTS cannot compare to uncooked gourmet desserts. There is a "realness" – a pure energy – to raw desserts that shines through in taste, color, and texture. The true testimony is how you feel after you eat them. Raw desserts are made of whole foods, whereas most conventional desserts are not. This means that our system recognizes their nutrition and does not trigger the 'craving' response that leads to overeating. Desserts containing highly processed and refined foods are stripped of the nutrition that exists in the original complete foods. Sensing this lack of nutrition the body creates the 'hunger' response because it is not getting the nourishment it requires. This vicious cycle can only be broken by eating nourishing whole foods in their most natural form.

Moderation with consumption of desserts is important for several reasons. Today's hybridized fruit is often too sweet. Many people have become addicted to it or have developed health issues like hypoglycemia, fungus and candida. Some of you may even be avoiding all sugar, including fruit, in order to allow your body to heal from certain health challenges. Let's face it; sugar feeds much more than just our sweet tooth. We all need to be careful how many sweets we eat, no matter what our health condition. In terms of food combining we also need to use caution. To get creative with fruit-based raw desserts, we add nuts or seeds, and that is not ideal food combining. Eat desserts occasionally or not at all. And when you do have dessert, consume it a minimum of 3 hours before or after any other conflicting foods you may have eaten that day.

You will be amazed to discover that any dessert you've ever had can be prepared uncooked! Raw desserts take a fraction of the time that conventional baking and pastries do. The recipes included here are a very small sample of what the world of living foods offers. Enjoy!

Carrot Spice Bars Ⓓ *(photo at left)*

YIELD: 12 BARS

2 cups roughly chopped carrot	1 teaspoon ground cinnamon
2 cups walnuts, soaked & dehydrated	½ teaspoon ground nutmeg
2 cups almonds, soaked & dehydrated	½ teaspoon ground ginger
½ cup dried pineapple, soaked & chopped	1 cup water
½ cup raisins, soaked	½ cup raisins, soaked
½ cup dates, pitted & soaked	½ cup chopped dried pineapple
1 teaspoon ground clove	½ cup chopped walnuts, soaked & dehydrated

1. In a mixing bowl, combine the carrot, 2 cups walnuts, almonds, first ½ cup pineapple, first ½ cup raisins, dates and spices. Toss together. Using a food processor, process this mixture until it is completely combined. Add the cup of water when processing to help the mixture move and process in the food processor.

2. To the processed mixture, stir in the remaining ingredients. Mix well and spread in a pan. Chill or freeze and frost with Tangy Cream "Cheeze" Frosting (p. 105).

Almond milk makes for a fulfilling and satisfying snack. Try these delicious versions with your favorite raw cookies.

Basic Almond Milk ⟩ *(see procedure on p. 35)*
Makes 6 cups

2 cups soaked almonds
6 cups filtered water
Mesh nut milk or sprouting bag

1. Blend soaked almonds in a high speed blender.

2. Using the nut milk bag, carefully strain the milk. With excess pulp, crumble on dehydrator sheets and dehydrate until crisp. Milk will last for 3 days in the fridge.

Almond Chai Latte
Makes 2 cups

2 cups basic almond milk (see above)	**¼ teaspoon nutmeg**
1½ tablespoons agave nectar[1]	**¼ teaspoon cardamom**
1 tablespoon mesquite powder	**½ tablespoon ginger juice**
1 teaspoon cinnamon	**Pinch of Celtic sea salt[2]**

Blend all ingredients in a high speed blender until smooth. If using whole ginger, you may need to strain before serving. Serve warm. Garnish with freshly grated cinnamon.

How to "Hippocratize" this recipe:
[1] Substitute stevia (to taste) for the agave nectar.
[2] Omit the Celtic sea salt.

Vanilla Mystic
Large serving

1¾ cups basic almond milk (see above)	**½ tablespoon coconut butter**
1 large piece coconut meat	**½ vanilla bean, chopped**
1 tablespoon agave nectar[1]	**Pinch of Celtic sea salt[2]**

Blend all ingredients in a high-speed blender until smooth. Be sure that coconut meat is thoroughly blended.

How to "Hippocratize" this recipe:
[1] Substitute stevia (to taste) for the agave nectar.
[2] Omit the Celtic sea salt.

Kitchen Tip! When making almond milk, be sure to save the pulp. Spread on dehydrator sheets to dry completely. Once dried, grind in high-speed blender to a silky flour, and store in an air-tight container for future use in breads and crackers.

Almond Milk *with* Brazil Nut *and* Date Cookies *and* Sugar-Free Cookies

Sugar-Free Cookies Ⓓ

YIELD: 24 COOKIES

4 cups nuts or seeds, soaked & dehydrated
4 - 5 tablespoons nut butter or sesame tahini

1 tablespoon ground cinnamon
10 - 15 drops liquid stevia extract

In a food processor, combine all ingredients and sweeten to taste. Add enough nut butter/ tahini to bring the mixture together. Form the mixture into desired shapes and dehydrate overnight or eat as is.

Brazil Nut and Date Cookies Ⓓ
YIELD: 25 COOKIES

4 cups Brazil nuts, soaked & dehydrated
2 cups dates, pitted & soaked

5 tablespoons raw carob powder
2 tablespoons ground cinnamon

1. In a food processor, chop the Brazil nuts coarsely. Place in a mixing bowl.

2. In a food processor, process the dates, carob, and cinnamon until a thick paste is formed; add to the nut mixture.

3. Combine the carob and cinnamon with date/nut mixture and hand mix until fully combined.

4. Form into desired cookie shape and dehydrate until desired doneness is achieved, or just refrigerate.

Blackberry Cobbler ⓓ

YIELD: 6 SERVINGS

2½ cups blackberries
4 - 5 tablespoons ground flax seed
2 tablespoons alcohol-free vanilla flavor
¼ teaspoon liquid stevia extract
2 cups blackberries
1 cup almonds, soaked & dehydrated

1 cup walnuts, soaked & dehydrated
1 cup sunflower seeds, soaked & dehydrated
½ cup soaked raisins
½ cup soaked dates
½ teaspoon ground cinnamon

1. In a food processor or blender, combine the 2½ cups blackberries, ground flax, vanilla and stevia. Blend or process until completely combined. Sweeten to taste. Stir in the remaining 2 cups blackberries. Put this filling in your glass serving dish.

2. In a food processor, combine the almonds, walnuts, sunflower seeds, raisins, dates and cinnamon. Process to form a crumbly, slightly sticky mixture. Sprinkle/spread this over the blackberry mixture in your dish. Dehydrate for 3-4 hours or until desired doneness is achieved. Serve warm.

Optional: Top with Maca Whipped Cream.

Low Sugar Truffles ⓓ

YIELD: 25 TRUFFLES

¾ cup raw almond butter
½ cup sunflower seeds, soaked,
   dehydrated and finely ground
¼ cup raw sesame tahini
¼ cup hemp seeds

¼ cup raw carob powder
1½ teaspoons ground cinnamon
½ teaspoon ground ginger
½ teaspoon ground nutmeg
2 tablespoons alcohol-free vanilla extract

In a mixing bowl, combine all ingredients. Mix well and season to taste. Form into balls and roll in additional hemp seeds and carob powder. Refrigerate or freeze and serve.

Sunny Raisin Cookies ⓓ

YIELD: 15 - 20 COOKIES

2 cups sunflower seeds, soaked & dehydrated
⅓ cup flax seeds, ground
1½ teaspoons psyllium husks powder
¾ teaspoon ground cinnamon or pumpkin
   pie spice

1 cup raisins, soaked in water
20 dates, pitted
1¼ cups soaking water from raisins
1 teaspoon alcohol-free vanilla extract

1. In a food processor, finely chop the sunflower seeds. Add the ground flax, psyllium powder, and spices. Set aside in a mixing bowl. Add the raisins.

2. In a blender, combine the dates, vanilla and soaking water from raisins (or just water). Blend well. Add to the mixing bowl and combine by hand with the sunflower-raisin mixture. Form into cookies and dehydrate overnight or until desired texture is achieved. Store in refrigeration because the cookies will not dry completely. Warm in the dehydrator before serving.

Tangy Cream "Cheeze" Frosting
YIELD: 2.5 CUPS

2 cups soaked pine nuts
½ cup dates, soaked
½ cup water

¼ cup fresh lemon juice
1 tablespoon alcohol-free vanilla flavor

In a blender, combine all ingredients. Blend very well. Use this to top your favorite bars or cookies.

Option: For an even creamier frosting, use a nut milk in place of the water.

Lemon Ice
YIELD: 2 SERVINGS

Water of one young coconut
1 lemon, juiced
5 drops liquid stevia extract

Blend or stir together all ingredients. Pour this mixture into an ice cream machine and freeze or pour into popsicle molds and freeze. Serve with fresh raspberries for a refreshing treat.

Maca Whipped Cream
YIELD: 2 CUPS

1 cup macadamia nuts, soaked & dehydrated
½ cup young coconut water or date soak water

5 dates, pitted & soaked
1 tablespoon coconut butter, optional

In a strong blender, combine all ingredients. Blend until smooth and creamy. Use as a topping for pies, beverages, puddings, etc.

Anna Maria's Favorite Raw Pie
YIELD: 1 PIE

Crust:
4 cups almonds, soaked
14 medjool dates, soaked

Filling:
4 bananas
1 cup dates, pitted & soaked
Garnish:
1 cup choice of papaya, mango, strawberry or other berries

1. Put in food processor and process until it will hold together in clumps. If not holding together, add a few more dates. Press into pie pan to make the "crust."

2. Process bananas with dates until creamy. This is the "sweetener" for the other fruits. Garnish and serve.

Variation:
• Add a little carob to the crust.

Note: The crust can be made without almonds and with soaked dates only for proper food combining.

Banana Ice Cream with Date Carob Sauce

YIELD: 4 CUPS

6 bananas, peeled & frozen

1. Using an appropriate juicer, process frozen bananas using the blank (homogenizing) attachment. They will come out looking and tasting like soft-serve ice cream.

2. For the sauce: In a blender, combine all ingredients and blend until smooth and creamy. Adjust the consistency of the sauce using water.

Sauce (yield 2 cups):
1 cup dates, soaked
½ vanilla bean, chopped
4 black olives, pitted
3 tablespoons raw carob powder
½ teaspoon ground cinnamon
1 cup water

Note: This sauce can be flavored in many other ways, such as using mint, orange, raspberry, strawberry, etc. You may also enjoy other fruit blended up as a sauce on this ice cream. Some other suggestions are strawberry, mango, pineapple or fresh berries.

Chilled Avocado Pudding

YIELD: 2-4 SERVINGS

1 avocado
12 dates, pitted & soaked

1 cup soak water from dates or coconut water
1 teaspoon cinnamon

Blend the avocado, dates and water until very smooth. Thin with water if necessary. Sprinkle cinnamon on top.

Options:
• Banana: add 1 banana
• Carob: add 1 banana, 1 tablespoon raw carob powder, and 3 black olives, (pitted)
• Mango: add half a mango, and use ½ cup orange juice as half the liquid

Raspberry Hazelnut Mousse

YIELD: 2 CUPS

1 cup raspberries
1 cup hazelnuts, soaked & dehydrated
½ cup soaked dates
1 tablespoon raw carob powder

½ cup date soak water or coconut water
1 tablespoon alcohol-free vanilla flavor
fresh mint leaves, raspberries, and
**   hazelnuts for garnish**

In a strong blender, combine all ingredients except garnishes. Blend very well, using a spatula to keep the mixture moving inside the blender. Sweeten to taste, chill and serve.

Note: This decadent creme goes very well with fresh berries, as a cream layer of a pie, or as a topping for your favorite dessert. It can also be frozen in an ice cream machine and makes a superb ice cream.

Trio of Tartlets[1] ⋏

Coconut tart crust
Makes 20-24 small tartlet shells

Crust:
1 cup macadamia nuts or cashews, raw
2 cups dried shredded coconut
¾-1 cup agave nectar
3 tablespoons lemon zest
1 teaspoon Celtic sea salt

For the tartlet:

1. Process all ingredients in a food processor until finely ground; it should form into a ball when pressed.

2. Line a small tartlet shell with plastic wrap and press 2+ tablespoons of dough in each.

3. Remove from tartlet shell and chill. Store in freezer.

To serve:

1. Serve on a rectangular plate, three tarts at a time. Top each with the below purées and select garnishes.

2. Finish the plate with a drizzle of fruit purée. Serve chilled.

Fillings:

Ginger-fig	Mango-Chile	Apricot-Citrus
1 cup dried figs, soaked for 2-4 hours then strained	**1 cup dried mango, soaked for 2-4 hours then strained**	**1 cup Turkish apricots, soaked for 2-4 hours then strained**
1 tablespoon lemon juice	**1 tablespoon lemon juice**	**2 tablespoons orange juice**
1 tablespoon grated ginger	**1 teaspoon agave nectar**	**2 tablespoons lemon zest**
½ teaspoon nutmeg	**½ teaspoon red Serrano chile, seeded and finely minced**	**1 tablespoon agave nectar**

Ginger-fig	Mango-Chile	Apricot-Citrus
Blend all ingredients in a food processor until smooth.	1. Process rehydrated mangos, lemon juice and agave in a food processor until smooth.	Process all ingredients in food processor until smooth.
Serve: 1½ tablespoons of purée on tartlet shell; garnish with candied ginger or fresh fig.	2. Fold in the minced chile.	**Serve:** 1½ tablespoons of purée on tartlet shell; garnish with citrus zest or small tangerine segment.
	Serve: 1½ tablespoons of purée on tartlet shell; garnish with mango or other tropical fruit relish.	

How to "Hippocratize" this recipe:

[1] In general, most desserts are not proper combinations and should be enjoyed only occasionally.

Pineapple Shortcake with Pineapple Sorbet and Candied Citrus Zest ⋏ Ⓓ

Pineapple Shortcake[1]

Makes two 9-inch cakes or 18-20 servings

6 cups carrots, shredded fine
3 cups dried pineapple, finely minced
2½ cups cashews, ground into flour[2]
3 cups dried coconut
1 tablespoon nutmeg, fresh grated
¼ cup agave nectar

¼ cup date paste
1 teaspoon vanilla extract
2 tablespoons orange zest
3 tablespoons mesquite powder
1 tablespoon Celtic sea salt

1. Place all ingredients into mixing bowl and hand-mix gently yet thoroughly; set aside.

2. Form cake into small 3-inch cylinder rounds. Dehydrate for 1 hour prior to serving.

To serve: On a plate, place shortcake in center and top with pineapple sorbet (see recipe below). Garnish plate with freshly diced pineapple or other finely diced tropical fruits.

How to "Hippocratize" this recipe:

[1] In general, most desserts are not proper combinations and should be enjoyed only occasionally.

[2] Substitute almonds or macadamia nuts for the cashews.

Pineapple Sorbet[1]

1 fresh pineapple, peeled and chopped
¼ cup agave nectar
3 tablespoons lemon juice
pinch of Celtic sea salt

1. Blend all ingredients in a high-speed blender until smooth.

2. Freeze in a square container.

3. Once frozen, slice into strips and/or cubes and process in food processor until sorbet consistency.

Note: For best quality sorbet, use the solid plate or blank "blade" of a single or twin gear juicer. Process frozen pineapple strips through the juicer.

How to "Hippocratize" this recipe:

[1] In general, most desserts are not proper combinations and should be enjoyed only occasionally.

Almond Butter and Rustic Jelly Sandwiches with Apple Cinnamon Bread[1] ⟩ ⓓ

Apple Cinnamon Bread

Makes two loaves: serves 8

3 sweet apples
1½ tablespoons almond butter
1½ tablespoons cinnamon
2 tablespoons agave nectar
3 soft dates, pitted

½ teaspoon Celtic sea salt
½ cup dried apples, very finely minced
1 cup flax meal, coarse
½ cup coconut flour*

1. Process the apple, almond butter, agave, dates and spices in a food processor until a smooth consistency is achieved.

2. While the processor is running, pour in the dried minced apples and the flax meal and coconut flour a tablespoon at a time until the mixture forms a ball. Note: If the mixture can roll into a ball by hand without sticking, no more flour is needed.

3. Form into a loaf and slice according to desired width. Dehydrate for about 4 hours. Bread will keep in the refrigerator for 1 week.

* To make coconut flour: Process dried coconut in high-speed blender or coffee grinder until finely ground.

For Almond Butter and Jelly Sandwiches

¼ cup almond butter
1 cup fresh raspberries
½ tablespoon lemon juice
1 tablespoon agave nectar

1. In a small bowl, add the raspberries, lemon and agave. Hand press the berries, forming a rustic 'jelly.'

2. On a slice of lightly warmed apple cinnamon bread, spread 2 tablespoons or so of almond butter; top with jelly. Serve open-faced and garnish with more chopped berries, or bananas.

How to "Hippocratize" this recipe:

[1] We consider this recipe a dessert. In general, most desserts are not proper combinations and should be enjoyed only occasionally.

Flourless Apple Spice Timbale with Cashew Maple Crème[1]

Serves 6

Cake:

2 cups fresh apples, shredded
1½ cups dried apple, minced
1½ cups raw pecans or walnuts, finely ground
1 cup dried shredded coconut
¼ cup currants or raisins
1½ cups soft dates, pitted and minced
1½ tablespoons cinnamon
1½ tablespoons orange zest
2½ tablespoons mesquite powder (optional)
1 teaspoon nutmeg
½ tablespoon Celtic sea salt

Garnish:

1 cup Cashew Maple Crème (see recipe below)
1 small bunch fresh currants for garnish

1. Place all cake ingredients into a mixing bowl and hand-mix gently yet thoroughly; set aside.

2. Using a small cylinder (or cake pan) press the 'cake batter' firmly in for desired thickness. Remove cylinder

3. Garnish with Cashew Maple Crème and finish with fresh berries or currants. Chill before serving.

Cashew Maple Crème with Citrus
Makes 2 cups

1½ cups whole raw cashews, soaked in filtered water for 4-6 hours, then strained[2]
½ cup liquid sweetener, pure maple syrup, agave nectar or date syrup
¼ cup fresh lemon juice
2 tablespoons cold-pressed coconut oil or coconut butter (optional)
½ teaspoon fresh vanilla bean, scraped, or 1 teaspoon pure alcohol-free vanilla extract
¼ teaspoon Celtic sea salt
2 tablespoons fresh lemon and lime zest

1. Blend the soaked cashews, liquid sweetener, fresh lemon juice, coconut oil, vanilla and sea salt in a high-speed blender. Note: Depending on the strength of the blender, you may need to add a bit of filtered water for desired consistency.

2. Once smooth, fold in the fresh citrus.

3. Chill and then, depending on the thickness, spread or drizzle on cake.

Kitchen Tip! Make extra apple cake for tasty granola bars; kids of all ages love them. Simply form the cake into small bars, place on dehydrator screens, and dehydrate at 110 degrees for 10-12 hours until dry. Keep in a sealed container.

How to "Hippocratize" this recipe:

[1] In general, most desserts are not proper combinations and should be enjoyed only occasionally.

[2] Substitute almonds, macadamia nuts, or pine nuts for the cashews.

Banana Cream Pie
YIELD: 1 PIE

Crust:
3 cups walnuts, soaked and dehydrated
¼ cup dates, pitted and soaked
½ teaspoon Bragg Liquid Aminos or pinch
  sea salt, optional

1. For the crust: Using a food processor, finely grind the walnuts to a crumble. Add the ¼ cup dates and Bragg Liquid Aminos or sea salt and process until combined. The mixture should be slightly sticky. Press the dough into a pie plate. Dehydrate overnight if a crunchy crust is desired.

Filling:
2 cups young coconut meat*
3 medium ripe bananas, broken in a few pieces
⅔ cup macadamia nuts, soaked
10 dates, pitted and soaked
2 tablespoons psyllium husks powder
½ cup of water of one young coconut
2 tablespoons alcohol-free vanilla extract,
  or ½ vanilla bean
4 ripe bananas, sliced

2. For the filling: In a strong blender, combine the coconut meat, bananas, macadamia nuts, 10 dates, psyllium, coconut water, and vanilla. Blend until very smooth and creamy. Stir in the sliced bananas and spread this filling evenly over the crust. For a nice finish, decorate the top of the pie with sliced bananas tossed in lemon juice (to slow browning) or other sliced fresh fruit. Chill and serve.

* Also known as "spoon meat." Young coconuts (green coconuts) can be found on trees all over the sub-tropics and tropics, especially South Florida. You may find them in local markets as well. If you cannot get coconuts, you may use 1¼ cup of pine or macadamia nuts (soaked).

Russian Rye Crisps

Dehydrates

CHAPTER II

THERE ARE MANY RECIPES THROUGHOUT THIS BOOK that can be dehydrated or easily converted into a delicious dehydrated recipe. These recipes are marked with the following symbol: **D** In this chapter, we provide a reference to these recipes as well as tips for easy dehydration. You can also learn more about the process of dehydration from the Basic Procedure chapter beginning on page 36.

Eating dehydrated food with fresh food (non-dehydrated) is always preferred. Have fun and experiment—you can't burn anything at 115 degrees!

Russian Rye Crisps *(photo at left)*
YIELD: 4 TRAYS

5 cups sprouted rye
2 cups chopped red onion
2 cups chopped green cabbage
3 tablespoons kelp powder
4 tablespoons dulse flakes
3½ cups water

Toppings:
dulse flakes
caraway seed
finely chopped red onion

In a blender, combine all ingredients except the toppings. Blend well until a thick batter is achieved. Pour onto a dehydrator tray using a teflex sheet or unbleached parchment paper beneath. Draw lines in the spread batter to "cut" the crackers. Sprinkle on desired toppings. Dehydrate overnight. Flip and dehydrate until completely dry and crisp.

Sugar-Free Cinnamon Pecans
YIELD: 6 CUPS

6 cups pecans, soaked
1½ tablespoons powdered stevia leaf
¼ cup water

1½ tablespoons ground cinnamon
2 tablespoons ground flax seed

1. In a small bowl, dissolve the stevia in the water.

2. Stir the soaked pecans into the stevia and water mixture.

3. In a bowl, combine the flax seed and cinnamon. Add this to the wet nut mixture and mix well. Let stand 20 minutes and mix again. Dehydrate.

Celery "Salt"
YIELD: 1 CUP

1 bunch celery

1. Slice the celery. The smaller you cut it, the faster it will dehydrate. Spread the slices out randomly over dehydrator trays. Dehydrate until completely dry.

2. When dry, use a spice grinder or dry blender container to process the celery to a fine powder. Store in an airtight container. Use just as you would salt, to enhance the flavor of your recipes or to sprinkle on your food.

Spicy Mixed Nuts

YIELD: 5 CUPS

5 cups of your favorite nuts or seeds *(for example)*:
1 cup pecans
1 cup walnuts
1 cup almonds
1 cup sunflower seeds
1 cup pumpkin seeds

2 - 4 tablespoons Bragg Liquid Aminos
  or Nama Shoyu
2 tablespoons ground flax seed
1½ teaspoons cayenne

1. Soak all nuts and seeds together overnight.

2. Drain and rinse the nuts. Set aside in a mixing bowl.

3. Add the Bragg Liquid Aminos or Nama Shoyu to the nuts and mix well.

4. In a separate small bowl, combine the ground flax and cayenne. Mix well. Then toss this with the wet nut mixture. Mix well.

5. Spread this mixture on dehydrator trays using a teflex sheet or unbleached parchment paper beneath. Dehydrate overnight or until completely dry. Store in an airtight container.

Mexiflax Crackers

YIELD: 4 TRAYS

1½ cups flax seed
2 cups ground flax seed
1 red bell pepper, chopped
½ red onion, chopped
½ bunch fresh cilantro, chopped
2 cloves garlic, chopped

1 tablespoon chili powder
1 teaspoon ground cumin
3 cups water
2 tablespoons Bragg Liquid Aminos
  or Nama Shoyu
1 tablespoon fresh lemon juice

1. In a bowl, combine the whole and ground flax seed. Set aside.

2. In a food processor, combine the red bell pepper, onion, cilantro, garlic, chili powder, cumin, Bragg Liquid Aminos or Nama Shoyu, and lemon juice. Process until a puree is achieved.

3. Stir the water into the flax seed bowl, then add the pureed mixture. Mix all ingredients very well. Let this mixture stand for at least 20 minutes, until it thickens.

4. Thinly spread the mixture on dehydrator trays, using a teflex sheet or unbleached parchment paper below. Draw lines (we recommend 6 rows x 6 rows) to cut the crackers. Dehydrate overnight. Flip and dehydrate until done. Store in air airtight container.

Note: See basic procedure for flax crackers on page 41.

Rosemary Garlic Croutons (or Veggie Flax Crackers) ⟩

Yields 8–9 dehydrator trays

2 cups golden flax seeds, soaked in 3 cups
   water for 4-6 hours
2 cups sunflower seeds (or almonds), soaked in
   water for 6-8 hours
3 carrots, chopped
2 cups celery, chopped
⅓ cup leek, chopped

1 cup red bell pepper, chopped
3 tablespoons rosemary, dried
2 tablespoons garlic powder or 3 cloves fresh garlic
2 tablespoons Italian seasoning, dried
½ teaspoon cayenne
1½ tablespoons Celtic sea salt[1]
Freshly cracked black pepper to taste[2]

1. In a food processor, blend the soaked flax and sunflower seeds until the mixture forms into a paté; there should be very few whole flax seeds. Place in large mixing bowl; set aside.

2. Process the remaining ingredients until finely minced or blended to a smooth consistency. Add to flax batch and mix thoroughly. Tip: mixing with your hands is much more effective than using a spoon.

3. Using a spatula, spread a half-inch even layer on each teflex sheet. When evenly spread, score 16 x 16, or increase the number of scores for smaller croutons.

4. Place in dehydrator and dehydrate at 110 degrees for 12 - 16 hours.**

5. Serve on top of Caesar salad or other salads as an extra. See page 48 for Caesar Salad recipe.

** **Important!** Halfway through the drying process, flip the teflex sheets onto the screens and peel them away; this will allow the underside of the food to dry thoroughly. Separate the croutons and continue drying until crunchy.

How to "Hippocratize" this recipe:

[1] Substitute dulse, Bragg Liquid Aminos, Nama Shoyu, kelp powder or celery powder for the Celtic sea salt.

[2] Substitute cayenne pepper for black pepper, or omit pepper entirely.

Rosemary Garlic Croutons are used in Simple Caesar Salad with Whole Leaf Dulse see page 48.

Pie Crust

YIELD: 1 CRUST

2 cups walnuts, soaked & dehydrated
2 cups pecans, soaked & dehydrated
⅓ cup soaked dates

In a food processor, combine the walnuts and pecans. Add any other dried, powdered spices you may desire (i.e. cinnamon, clove, ginger, etc.) Process this mixture to a fine crumble.

Note: See basic procedure for pie crust/cookies on pages 32-34.

Sweet Potato Chips
YIELD: 4 TRAYS

3 sweet potatoes
¼ cup Bragg Liquid Aminos or Nama Shoyu

1. Scrub the sweet potatoes; do not peel.

2. Thinly slice the sweet potatoes using a mandoline or other thin slicer. We prefer the Kyocera ceramic hand slicer (available at the Hippocrates store) for this.

3. In bowl, toss the sliced sweet potato with the Bragg Liquid Aminos or Nama Shoyu. Allow to stand at least 15 minutes.

4. Lay the slices out on dehydrator trays using teflex or unbleached parchment paper beneath. You may place them very close together, as they will only get smaller. Dehydrate overnight or until desired crispness is achieved. Store in an airtight container.

Note: See basic procedure for vegetable chips on page 39.

Nori Nuggets
YIELD: 45 - 60 NUGGETS

2 cups pumpkin seeds, soaked
1 cup chopped carrot
¾ cup chopped fresh cilantro, optional
½ cup chopped scallion
2 tablespoons chopped fresh ginger
2 cloves garlic, chopped

2 tablespoons fresh lemon juice
1½ tablespoons Bragg Liquid Aminos or Nama Shoyu
1 tablespoon water
15 nori sheets

1. In a food processor, combine the soaked pumpkin seeds, carrot, cilantro, scallion, ginger, garlic, lemon juice, Bragg Liquid Aminos or Nama Shoyu, and water. Process this mixture until it becomes a thick paste. (You may use any paté or thick dip in place of this mixture.)

2. Place a thin line of paté towards one end of the nori sheet (See Basic Procedure on pages 28-29 for an illustration of Nori Rolls.) Roll the nori up around the paté and continue to roll. The completed roll should be about 1 inch in diameter.

3. Dehydrate the rolls overnight and cut into 1½ inch chunks. Continue to dehydrate until desired texture is achieved. Store in an airtight container.

Apple Snacks

YIELD: 6 TRAYS

4 apples, cored
fresh lemon juice, as needed

1 teaspoon ground cinnamon
¼ teaspoon ground clove

1. Wash the apples; core but do not peel.

2. Thinly slice the apples using a mandoline or other thin slicer. We prefer the Kyocera ceramic hand slicer (available at the Hippocrates store) for this.

3. In bowl, toss the sliced apple with some lemon juice.

4. Lay the apple slices on dehydrator trays using a teflex sheet or unbleached parchment paper beneath. Sprinkle the apples evenly with the cinnamon and clove. Dehydrate overnight or until desired texture is achieved. Store in an airtight container.

Note: See basic procedure for fruit chips on page 38.

Sprouted Grain Pizza Crust

YIELD: 1 CRUST

2 cups dry kamut grain
1 tablespoon psyllium husks powder or
  ground flax seed

1 teaspoon kelp powder
1½ cups water
4 drops liquid stevia extract

1. Soak and sprout the kamut. You may use any other grain in place of kamut.

2. In a mixing bowl, combine all ingredients. Transfer this mixture to a blender. You may need to separate it into 2 batches. Blend very well until a thick batter is achieved.

3. Pour this mixture out onto a dehydrator tray using a teflex sheet or unbleached parchment paper beneath. You may choose to make it into one large round, 2 medium sized rounds, or smaller personal-pizza sized rounds. No matter the size round you use, spread the batter evenly and thickly to achieve a somewhat chewy, doughy crust.

4. Dehydrate overnight. Flip and dehydrate further until desired texture is achieved. Sauce with Raw Red Pepper Marinara (see recipe on page 53) and top with your favorite chopped vegetables and sprouts. For an even more cooked appeal, you may even choose to dehydrate it further once the toppings are added.

Note: See basic procedure for pizza crust on page 42.

The following dehydrated recipes have been modified from the original raw recipes. Please refer to the page number listed for recipe ingredients and follow these instructions for creating a wonderful dehydrated version.

Caraway Carrot Rye Crackers

See recipe for Caraway Carrot Rye on page 71
YIELD: 4 TRAYS

1. Prepare this recipe without the oil.

2. Blend all ingredients using enough water to achieve a thick batter.

3. Spread the mixture on dehydrator trays using a teflex sheet or unbleached parchment paper beneath. Score lines in the cracker batter to "cut" the crackers. Dehydrate overnight. Flip and dehydrate until completely dry. Store in an airtight container.

Mexicali Quinoa Crackers

See recipe for Mexicali Quinoa on page 68
YIELD: 4 TRAYS

1. Prepare this recipe without the oil and transfer it to a blender.

2. Blend well, using only enough water to produce a thick batter. Spread this mixture on dehydrator trays, using a teflex sheet or unbleached parchment paper beneath. Score lines in the batter to "cut" the crackers. Dehydrate overnight. Flip and dehydrate until completely dry. Store in an airtight container.

Lite Chickpea Crackers

See recipe for Cauliflower Garbanzo Italienne on page 70
YIELD: 4 TRAYS

1. Prepare this recipe without the oil and transfer it to a blender.

2. Blend well, using only enough water to produce a thick batter. Spread this mixture on dehydrator trays, using a teflex sheet or unbleached parchment paper beneath. Score lines in the batter to "cut" the crackers. Dehydrate overnight. Flip and dehydrate until completely dry. Store in an airtight container.

Veggie Spelt Crackers

See recipe for Spelt Surprise on page 70
YIELD: 2 TRAYS

1. Prepare this recipe without the oil and transfer it to a blender.

2. Blend well, using only enough water to produce a thick batter. Spread this mixture on dehydrator trays, using a teflex sheet or unbleached parchment paper beneath. Score lines in the batter to "cut" the crackers. Dehydrate overnight. Flip and dehydrate until completely dry. Store in an airtight container.

Quiche Crust

See recipe for Wild Mushroom Quiche on page 82
YIELD: 1 CRUST

Prepare only the crust from this recipe. Dehydrate overnight. Fill with your choice of quiche filling or other vegetable mixture.

Hearty Brazil Nut Crackers

See recipe for Brazil Nut Loaf on page 86
YIELD: 4 TRAYS

Note: Refer to basic procedure for Savory Crackers on page 41.

Sunny Onion Crackers

See recipe for Sunny Onion Dressing on page 47
YIELD: 4 TRAYS

1. Prepare the Sunny Onion Dressing recipe, but increase the quantity of sunflower seeds by ¼-½ cup, depending on how thick you want your crackers to be. Blend well.

2. Spread this mixture on dehydrator trays, using a teflex sheet or unbleached parchment paper beneath. Score lines in the batter to "cut" the crackers. Dehydrate overnight. Flip and dehydrate until completely dry. Store in an airtight container.

Dehydrated Salads

With the exception of those using avocado, most salads are excellent dehydrated. Below is a list of our favorite salads for dehydrating. Prepare them without oil and then dehydrate until completely dry. Store in an airtight container.

See recipes for:
Beet Onion Salad on page 96
Dulse Italiano on page 98
Sea Lettuce Salad on page 96

YIELD: 3 TRAYS

Sea Vegetable Salad on page 98
Seafood Salad on page 99
Sesame Julienne on page 96
Squash Ratatouille on page 95

Other Dehydrated Goodies

Below is a list of some of our favorite recipes from other chapters that taste great either raw or dehydrated. None of the recipes noted below need modification for dehydration. Enjoy them either way!

Sugar-Free Cookies see recipe on page 103
Stuffed Mushrooms see recipe on page 84
Stuffed Zucchini see recipe on page 68
Nutmeat Loaf see recipe on page 85
Marinated Onions see recipe on page 89

Pineapple Shortcake see recipe on page 108
Apple Cinnamon Bread see recipe on page 109
Blackberry Cobbler see recipe on page 104
Brazil Nut and Date Cookies see recipe on page 103

Glossary

Acidulated Water: water with a splash of lemon juice (most commonly). It can also be made by adding lime or grapefruit juice to water. Acidulated water slows the oxidation and the resulting discoloration of foods.

Adzuki or Aduki: a small, red, highly nutritious and easily digestible bean. Sprouted adzuki beans are excellent for kidney health, among other things.

Alcohol-Free Vanilla Extract/Flavor: vanilla bean that has been steeped in glycerin rather than alcohol, to extract flavor and preserve it.

Almond Meal: dried almond "pulp," left over from making almond milk. When you squeeze or strain almond milk, you are left with the more fibrous part of the chopped up almonds. We like to dehydrate this and save it for use in other recipes, such as patés, "cheeses," salads and/or pie crusts.

Amaranth: a tiny seed native to South America and southern Asia. Amaranth is treated like a grain and contains high amounts of the more rare amino acids, lysine and methionine. Amaranth is great for sprouting or a healthy cooked grain.

Apple Pectin: a soluble fiber derived from apples that has a gel-forming effect when mixed with water.

Arame: a tough member of the kelp family—this seaweed is typically cut into very thin strips and then dried, steamed or boiled to soften. Hydrate it by soaking in room temperature water for 5-10 minutes before using.

Avocado: a rich buttery fruit (although not sweet) native to Central America. Many varieties of avocados exist. Most common are Haas (smaller, fattier and very dark-skinned when ripe) and Florida (large, green-skinned and lighter in taste and texture) avocados. Avocados ripen off the tree. When ripe, an avocado should give just slightly to the touch. Avocados are rich in healthy fats and Vitamin E.

Black Radish: a member of the radish family, larger than red radishes, with an outer black skin and inner white flesh.

Bragg Liquid Aminos: an unfermented soy sauce made only from organic soybeans and water. Use Bragg Liquid Aminos as a flavor enhancer and salt substitute.

Buckwheat: a triangular alkaline seed that is treated like a grain. Buckwheat is available in unhulled (for green sprouts) and toasted (kasha) and raw hulled forms. Sprout hulled buckwheat and then dehydrate it for a crunchy cereal or salad addition. Sprout unhulled buckwheat for growing into buckwheat sprouts/lettuce. Buckwheat is high in rutin (very good for the circulatory system) and other B vitamins, and has mucilagenic properties soothing to the digestive tract.

Buckwheat Sprouts: also known as buckwheat greens or lettuce, this refers to the growing of an actual leafy sprout several inches tall. With its lime green leaves and reddish stems, buckwheat sprouts are great for salads.

Burdock Root: supreme for the blood, burdock root is a long, thin, hairy brownish root. The flesh is off-white in color and oxidizes rapidly once cut (use acidulated water to slow oxidation). The flavor of burdock is very earthy. Shred it, juice it, slice or julienne it.

Carob: the pod of a Mediterranean evergreen tree, also known as "locust bean." Carob powder is made from the dehydrated pulp of the pod. It is most often used in raw desserts, due to its sweet nature and likeness to chocolate. Look for raw carob powder, as opposed to roasted (much darker in color).

Celery Root: a large, hairy, round root otherwise known as celeriac. It is indeed the root of the celery stalk. Its flesh is cream colored and has a very fresh, crisp taste. Treat cut celery root with acidulated water to prevent browning. Shred, slice or juice it.

Chickpea: also known as the garbanzo bean, chickpeas are large and yellow-brown in color. They can be sprouted and eaten raw just as they are, or blended to make hummus and other dips or sauces.

Chiffonnade: an extremely thin, ribbon-like cut of a leafy vegetable or herb done by hand or vegetable slicer.

Chili Powder: a generic blend of spices typically including cumin, oregano, coriander, garlic, allspice, cloves and sometimes cayenne. Chili powders vary in spiciness, so check yours before adding to a recipe. All our recipes were made with Frontier Chili Powder.

Chinese Five Spice: a spice blend containing cinnamon, fennel, clove, anise and white pepper.

Courgette: a small summer squash or zucchini.

Daikon: a large white root similar in shape to a carrot but usually much larger. When fresh it is very crisp, juicy and mildly sweet. Daikon radishes are typically milder in spiciness than standard red radishes.

Dehydrated Crackers: crackers that have been made from a thinly spread blended or ground up mixture and dehydrated to achieve a crunchy snack. Crackers may consist of any type of vegetables mixed with either a sprouted grain, nut, or seed.

Dehydrator: a piece of equipment used to gently remove water from food (dehydrate it) in an effort to preserve, change textures, concentrate flavors, gently warm food and/or add more creativity to a raw foods program. Excalibur® is our favorite brand. Use your dehydrator to create everything from cookies to crackers and fruit leather or pizza.

Dice: to cut a vegetable or fruit into small cubes. In general, a diced piece measures roughly ¼ to ½ inch on each side.

Drain: to remove the water from a soaking item of food. Pour your soaking items into a colander, and let the water drain off, or cover the top of your jar or container with a mesh screen, and then invert it, allowing water to run out.

Dried Fruit: any fruit that has been dehydrated and can be stored for long periods of time. The sugar becomes very concentrated in dried fruit, so always use in moderation and soak in water before consuming. Be sure to look for dried fruit without preservatives, particularly sulfur.

Dulse: a dark, purplish-red seaweed harvested mainly on the North Atlantic Coast. This soft seaweed is very high in minerals and can be purchased in whole leaf form, flakes or granules. Dehydrate whole leaf dulse for a crunchy crispy snack.

Enzyme: chemical protein complexes with life force that enable natural body processes. Food enzymes assist in the digestion of a particular food. Enzymes are necessary in all life processes. Their presence is a significant difference in the distinction between raw and cooked foods.

Enzyme Inhibitors: chemical protein complexes that prevent the action of enzymes, thus making thorough digestion difficult or impossible.

Fenugreek: a triangular, yellowish-brown seed with unique liver-cleansing properties.

Finely Diced: cut into very small cubes, roughly ⅛ to ¼ inch in size.

Flax: a small brown or golden seed with very unique gelatinous properties. Proportionally rich in Omega-3, 6, and 9 fatty acids, flax seed is highly perishable once ground or processed. Use your spice grinder to grind it fresh every time. Ground flax seed makes an excellent salad sprinkle or a thickener for liquids, smoothies, soups, and patés.

Fucus: a brown seaweed with narrow fronds. Fucus is often difficult to find, but it's a delicious mineral-rich treat in salads and as a snack.

Garbanzo: Also known as the chick pea, garbanzo beans are medium-sized and yellow-brown in color. Garbanzo beans can be sprouted and eaten raw just as they are, or blended to make hummus and other dips or sauces.

Golden Beet: a vibrant golden-yellow fleshed beet. The skin of golden beets is typically bright orange to brown in color. Golden beets oxidize rapidly when cut, so dousing them with some lemon water helps retain the color. Shred them, slice them for chips, blend them into a soup, or use a little in your juice.

Green Wrap: a wrap that uses a large green leaf to contain other ingredients, such a sprouts, paté, avocado or other vegetables. This is the raw foodist's answer to the standard flour tortilla wrap.

Hemp Seeds: highly nutritious small white and green disks that are rich in protein. When blended, hemp seeds are extremely creamy. Add them to your salad or favorite dressings and soups.

Herbs de Provence: an herbal blend used for flavoring consisting of winter savory, thyme, rosemary, basil, tarragon and lavender flowers.

Hijiki or Hiziki: another tough member of the kelp family, this seaweed comes in thin, wavy, blackish-brown pieces. Hijiki is high in minerals and should be soaked in room-temperature water to soften it before use. Hijiki is sometimes cooked in the processes of harvesting and packaging.

Homogenize: to grind and combine thoroughly, achieving a uniform mixture, using a blender or juicer.

Homogenizing Attachment: this varies depending on the type of juicer you have, but typically is a solid plastic plate or casing used for thorough grinding of a mixture or product. Consult your juicer manual if you have difficulty determining which attachment is the homogenizer.

Hulled: this term means that the outer husk or protective layer (hull) of a grain, bean or seed is removed. The hull is indigestible but has value when it comes to sprouting certain things. Not all grains/beans have a removable hull.

Italian Seasoning: an herbal blend of oregano, marjoram, thyme, rosemary, basil and sage.

Jerusalem Artichoke: another name for the sunchoke, Jerusalem artichokes look similar to ginger root in that they are small, knotty, brown-skinned roots. They are great shredded or thinly sliced and taste like a potato with a slightly nutty flavor. Jerusalem artichokes oxidize (turn brown) very rapidly after cutting, so use acidulated water to preserve them if necessary.

Juicer: a tool used to separate the liquid content from the fiber content of a plant. Juicers remove the pulp so that you may drink the liquid nutrition of whatever you are juicing. There are many types of juicers and not all are created equally. We recommend a Twin-Gear Juicer for its versatility and its ability to obtain a high yield of juice, retain nutrients and effectively juice a wide range of items.

Julienne: a thin matchstick cut of a vegetable or fruit. Generally speaking, a julienne cut item measures ⅛ inch x ⅛ inch x 1½ inch long.

Kamut: an ancient Egyptian form of wheat that contains less gluten than ordinary wheat. This grain can be grown for juicing grass (like wheatgrass), sprouted for use in grain crackers and salads.

Kelp: a highly mineralized sea vegetable, available in powder, granules or whole leaf form. Kelp powder is a great flavor enhancer and salt substitute.

Kohlrabi: a member of the cabbage family, kohlrabi has a round bulbous end with leaves shooting out from its sides. Although it seems like a root vegetable, technically it is not. You will find kohlrabi in white, purple, or green and can use the stem as you would any root vegetable. The leaves are also edible.

Large-Diced: cutting vegetable/fruit into large cubes one inch in size.

Liquid Stevia Extract: a form of stevia, this clear liquid mixes into preparations very easily without discoloring them. We like the one made by the Stevita Company.

Marinate: the process of allowing a food to sit in a seasoned liquid, typically consisting of an acid, oil, salt and flavorings/seasonings. Marinating softens food and infuses flavor, often providing a seemingly cooked product.

Mexican Seasoning: a spice blend typically containing chili peppers, garlic, onion, paprika, cumin, celery seed, oregano and bay.

Millet: a small, round, alkaline grain. Millet is available in hulled (for cooking) and unhulled (for sprouting) forms. Sprouted millet makes great crackers and salads, while hulled millet makes an excellent cooked cereal grain.

Mung Bean: a small, green, easy to digest bean. Mung beans can be sprouted and used raw as a sprouted bean, or can be grown longer in the dark to make 2-3 inch translucent "bean sprouts"—typically used in the preparation of Chinese foods.

Nama Shoyu: a form of soy sauce, this fermented liquid is unpasteurized and used where flavor enhancement (salt) may be desired. It does contain wheat.

Nori: a seaweed that is typically pressed into paper-thin sheets for rolling sushi or other items. Nori is also available (although harder to find) in whole leaf form. Sheets of nori are available toasted (also known as "sushi nori") and raw, so look for the untoasted nori sheets.

Nori Roll: a cylindrical food roll made by taking a sheet of nori seaweed, rolling ingredients inside, and then sealing it with water. Most people recognize nori from Japanese sushi restaurants, where it is most commonly found.

Nut Loaf: a smooth, rich, typically well-seasoned mixture of vegetables, flavorings, and most commonly, nuts and/or seeds. Nut loaves (or patés) are processed using a food processor, either a twin-gear or a single-auger juicer which homogenizes (recommended.) The mixture is then shaped into a loaf.

Nut or Seed Butter: a paste made from finely ground nuts or seeds. Always look for raw nut/seed butters, or make your own. The less oil separation, the fresher the product.

Oxidation or Oxidize: a reaction, often marked by a discoloration of food, that occurs when a substance comes in contact with oxygen. In terms of food, oxidation is not desirable.

Paté: a smooth, rich, typically well-seasoned mixture of vegetables, flavorings and, most commonly, nuts and/or seeds. Patés are processed using either a food processor or a juicer which homogenizes (recommended), as do most twin gear and single auger juicers.

Pizza Seasoning: a spice blend containing dehydrated onion, fennel, oregano, basil, dehydrated garlic, bell peppers, chilies, marjoram, parsley, thyme, celery flakes. We love the Frontier™ brand of pizza seasoning.

Poultry Seasoning: a spice blend containing sage, thyme, dehydrated onion, marjoram, black pepper, celery seed and red pepper.

Psyllium: a plant prized for its high fiber content. We use psyllium husks powder as a thickening agent in raw foods. A little goes a long way and it does take time for its full thickening potential to be reached.

Pumpkin Pie Spice: a spice blend containing cinnamon, ginger, nutmeg and cloves.

Quinoa: a high-protein grain native to South America. Shaped like small flat disks, quinoa sprouts extremely rapidly and makes for great salads and crackers.

Raw Sesame Tahini: a thick paste made of ground-up raw sesame seeds. Tahini is used in dressings, sauces and hummus and as a binder in burgers and nut balls.

Rutabaga: a large round, tan root. Rutabaga is mild in flavor and can be shredded or thinly sliced and added to any salad or other savory raw food preparation.

Rye: a hearty grain used for sprouting and growing grass. Sprouted rye makes great dehydrated crackers, raw pilafs and salads.

S-blade: the standard blade of a food processor. It is shaped somewhat like the letter "S," with a curved blade protruding from each side of a centerpiece. When you purchase a food processor, this is the blade that always comes with it.

Sauerkraut: a fermented, shredded cabbage product. Raw sauerkraut is excellent for digestive and intestinal health.

Sea Lettuce: a delicate green seaweed with a high mineral content. Sea lettuce is great dried or wet.

Sea Palm: variety of seaweed harvested in the Pacific.

Sea Vegetable Salad Mix: a packaged blend of sea vegetables that needs only brief hydration and is ready to use. We love the one made by Soken company. Osawa also makes a nice one.

Shred: to cut a vegetable using either a hand grater or shredding attachment of a food processor to make small thin strips.

Single Auger Juicer: a juicer with one rotating auger that crushes vegetables and fruits against a screen, extracting the juice.

Soak: to cover a food with plenty of water to begin the germination process or simply to hydrate. Always soak in pure water.

Spelt: less adulterated, ancient relative of wheat. This grain can be used just like wheat; for grass, sprouting, crackers, salads or stuffings.

Spiralizer: a hand-operated tool excellent for taking any round vegetable and turning it into long strands or slices. A spiralizer is used to make raw pastas and other thin slices of everything from zucchini and sweet potatoes to radishes and beets. We recommend the Benriner® Turning Vegetable Slicer.

Sprout: soaking a bean, seed, grain or nut activates its dormant life force and begins the germination process, activating its enzymes. The term "sprout" can mean anything from a sprouted rye seed to a leafy sunflower sprout.

Sprouted Grain: a grain seed (such as wheat, rye, kamut or spelt) that has been soaked and sprouted so that is has a "tail" $\frac{1}{16}$ to $\frac{1}{4}$ inch long. It is completely edible in this raw state.

Stevia: a South American herb with an extremely sweet taste, but no actual sugar or calories. Stevia is appropriate for everyone as a sweetener, especially for those with sugar aversions of any kind. It is 200-300 times sweeter-tasting than standard white sugar but does not produce a glycemic response. It is available in powder or liquid form.

Sunchoke: another name for the Jerusalem artichoke, sunchokes are small, knotty, brown-skinned roots that resemble ginger root. They are good shredded or thinly sliced and are like a potato with a slightly nutty flavor. Sunchokes oxidize (turn brown) very rapidly after cutting, so use acidulated water to preserve if necessary.

Sunflower Sprout: the leafy sprout grown from unhulled sunflower seeds. Sunflower sprouts are high in complete protein and, overall, a powerhouse of nutrition. Add them to any salad or juice.

Tahini: a thick paste or seed butter made from ground sesame seeds. Look for raw sesame tahini rather than roasted sesame tahini.

Teff: the tiniest grain of all, teff is native to Ethiopia. It can be sprouted (it does best on a moist towel), or used for cooking.

Teflex Sheet: a reusable sheet made by the Excalibur® Company for use on its dehydrator trays. These sheets fit the trays perfectly and are used under any item that would normally stick or drip through the mesh screen of the trays. Any food item comes off of these sheets very easily and they can be reused for years.

Turmeric: a tropical root related to ginger, this vibrant yellow-orange root is available fresh or in the powdered form (most common). It has a bitter taste and is very high in antioxidants, having powerful healing properties. Turmeric is what typically gives certain curry powders or pastes the intense yellow color and does stain surfaces very easily.

Turnip: a white-fleshed root native to cooler weather climates. Turnips can be shredded, sliced thin for chips, or added as an ingredient in nut loaves or patés.

Twin Gear Juicer: a juicer that has two spinning gears or augers that gently squeeze foods to produce juice or a finely ground pulp. Most twin gear juicers also have magnets in the gears to help prolong the retention of nutrients after the grinding/squeezing process has taken place.

Unhulled: this term means that the hull, or protective outer husk, of a grain, bean or seed has been left on and intact. It refers to seeds in their completely unprocessed state. This is desirable for sprouting certain items.

Waffle-Sliced: a vegetable/fruit cut made by a mandolin (a kitchen gadget that makes a variety of food slices and shapes) or vegetable slicer with a waffle (wavy, undulating-edged) blade.

Wakame: a variety of seaweed that is available in whole leaf on the stem, flakes or pieces. Typically, wakame is soaked in water before using. Like most seaweeds, it is high in minerals.

Wasabi: a Japanese horseradish that is typically dried to a powder and mixed with water to form a paste. Wasabi classically accompanies sushi and is extremely hot and cleansing to the sinuses. Look for wasabi powders or pastes without artificial coloring or preservatives.

Young Coconut Meat: the inner jelly-like layer of flesh inside a young (green or yellow) coconut. This meat is easier to digest than mature coconut meat and can typically be scraped out with a spoon, thus its other name, "spoon meat." Blended, this spoon meat makes an excellent creamy base for dressings, soups and dessert creams and sauces.

Young Coconut Water: the liquid found inside a young coconut. Typically these coconuts are green to yellow on the outside. This water is highly nutritious and full of electrolytes.

Index

Resources

HIPPOCRATES STORE
(561) 471-8876 ext 2124 or 2171
Toll-free 1-877-582-5850
www.HippocratesInstitute.org
Juicers, dehydrators, teflex sheets, books, prepared raw food products, sprout bags, sprouting equipment, seeds, wheatgrass, and supplements

DOOR-TO-DOOR ORGANICS
(888) 283-4443
www.doortodoororganics.com
Mail order and home delivery organic produce

ESSENTIAL LIVING FOODS
(310) 319-1555
www.essentiallivingfoods.com
Conscious consumerism, organic nuts, olives, dried fruit, oils, herbs

GOLD MINE NATURAL FOODS
(800) 475-3663
www.goldminenaturalfoods.com
Organic sea veggies, seeds, nuts, ceramic knives, olives and Nama Shoyu

GOT SPROUTS
(561) 689-9464
www.gotsprouts.com
Quality certified organic wheat seeds and wheatgrass, sprouts, juicers, seed and growing supplies—delivery and shipping available

HAPPY COW
www.happycow.net
The most trusted vegetarian and vegan restaurant guide since 1999

JAFFE BROTHERS (Wholesale only)
(760) 749-1133
www.organicfruitsandnuts.com
Organic dried fruit, nuts, seeds, olives, nut butters and raw carob

JOHNNY'S SELECTED SEEDS
www.johnnyseeds.com
Vegetable seeds; medicinal and culinary herb seeds; flower seeds; cover crops, farm seed, and pasture mixes; fruit plants and seeds, and high quality, problem-solving tools and supplies

MAINE COAST SEA VEGETABLES
(207) 565-2907
www.seaveg.com
Dulse, kelp, kombu, sea lettuce and other sea vegetables

OMEGA NUTRITION
(800) 661-FLAX (3529)
www.omeganutrition.com
Oils, oil capsules and nutritional products

PALM BEACH ORGANICS
www.palmbeachorganics.org
Organic fruits and veggie buying group sourced from farms within the continental USA with a focus on Florida grown

PALM BEACH ORGANICS
www.palmbeachorganics.org
Organic fruits and veggie buying group sourced from farms within the continental USA with a focus on Florida grown

UNIVERSAL LIVING SPROUTS
(561) 795-2554
www.ulsprouts.com
Quality certified organic wheat seeds and wheatgrass, sprouts, and seeds—delivery and shipping available

Welcome to the possibility of optimal health and vibrant living! For more than 50 years, Hippocrates Health Institute has helped hundreds of thousands of people reclaim their health and regain their joy and passion for life. Many of our guests come to us with serious and life-threatening illnesses, while others come simply because they wish to live free from strife and disease. Whatever your reason for joining us, our commitment remains the same: to provide the highest quality education and the most advanced tools for conscious and inspired living, all within a supportive, loving and natural environment. Hippocrates' program is founded on the belief that a pure enzyme-rich diet, proper exercise, positive thinking and noninvasive therapies combined with appropriate  supplementation are the essential elements of healthful living. While the thousands of testimonials from our guests speak for themselves, we are proud to have been recognized by Spa Magazine as the #1 Medical Wellness Spa in the world. Now we invite you, in the course of the next several pages, to get to know Hippocrates and learn how our programs, products and services can be of assistance to you and those you love.

Yours in Health,
Drs. Brian and Anna Maria Clement

In addition to delicious organic raw and living foods, daily exercise programs including yoga, Chi Kung and fitness classes, and a multitude of spa and salon services, Hippocrates offers some of the most highly specialized and advanced natural health technologies and therapies available today. Our 50-acre tropical facility offers ozonated pools, infrared saunas, ONDAMED, CyberScan, arteriography, cold laser, magnetic & Turbosonic treatments, exercise classes, wheatgrass & juice therapies, and optional therapies such as oxygen, cranial electrotherapy stimulation, aqua chi, bone evaluation and whole food IVs. Upon arriving, guests meet with our experienced staff of nutritionists, doctors, nurses and health professionals and receive a personalized health program designed to help you get the most from your stay. Nearly everyone who visits Hippocrates comes with a desire to change something about the way they are living, which is why we call our signature program the "Life Transformation" program. Whatever change you desire, know that you will create it, and more, through this astounding experience.

Here's what some of our guests had to say about their experience:

" I have maintained the program for the last ten years during which time my weight has regulated, a lump disappeared, the polyp on my vocal chord is almost non-existent, my surgery for gingivitis was no longer necessary, and my hypoglycemia has come under control. Thank you Hippocrates, now I have the love and serenity in life that I had been searching for."

– Sietske Tyte

"A decade ago I was diagnosed with cancer. Today, as best as modern medicine can tell, there is no evidence of cancer in my body. With the support of this lifestyle, I am now looking forward to a long life full of good times and health."

– Lilli B. Link, M.D.

"When I was given a death sentence by the physician who discovered pancreatic cancer in my body, I attended Hippocrates, healed myself and saw a multitude of others recover from a wide variety of cancers and other diseases."

– Samantha Young

3-Week Life Transformation Program

Our signature program provides you with the tools and information to restore physical, mental and emotional health and achieve the highest levels of personal well being. The Hippocrates' food & juice program, featuring highly-nutritious organic raw and living foods, detoxifies and cleanses the body on a cellular level, allowing the body to heal and rebuild from the inside out, naturally. Through daily classes and lectures, you learn the science behind the lifestyle program that many call "miraculous." You also gain valuable information on transitioning to a healthy lifestyle while experiencing first-hand the many therapies and practices such as massage, colon hydrotherapy, exercise and contemplation that assist you in creating vibrant health. The Hippocrates program, practiced successfully by thousands now for decades, has overwhelmingly resulted in short and long term symptom relief and in many cases the complete elimination of disease and illness.

The 3-week Hippocrates Life Transformation Program begins every Sunday and ends on a Saturday, and is offered continuously throughout the year. One week is the minimum stay.

The Health Educator Program
9-Week Program

Hippocrates Health Educator Program is for people who desire an extended, in-depth experience of and education in raw and living food nutrition and the Hippocrates' Lifestyle. This comprehensive immersion program provides a detailed introduction to key components of the Hippocrates' Lifestyle, including: anatomy & physiology, enzymatic nutrition, sprouting, food preparation, natural therapies, and more. It is an essential program for anyone wishing to add to his or her own personal knowledge of the living foods lifestyle, or for integration into a natural health career.

This 9-week Intensive Program is offered three times per year in the Spring, Summer and Fall.

Save Your Life! 2-hour Lecture Series

Last Wednesday of every month at Hippocrates Health Institute.

- Learn how to increase energy, and build strength and vitality through the Hippocrates' Life Transformation program.
- Hear valuable strategies for creating health and for preventing and recovering from threatening illnesses.
- Enjoy a complimentary Hippocrates' food tasting.

For information and reservations on any of these programs call 800.842.2125 or visit our website www.hippocratesinst.org

The Hippocrates Health Series...
Bring the Life Transformation experience into your home

This extraordinary audio/visual series introduces you to the principles of the Hippocrates Program which have been the foundation for healthy and successful living for more than 50 years. The Hippocrates Life Transformation Programs are proven to consistently restore vitality and improve overall quality of life. Weight reduction, pain relief and recovery from serious life-threatening illnesses are just some of the many results that guests have achieved. Now, the secrets of this program are yours to enjoy at home! Some of the topics covered in this comprehensive series are:

- Digestion and elimination
- Supplements, Algae, Herbs and Homeopathy
- Food Combining
- Fasting
- Emotional and spiritual healing
- Detoxification

Plus! Your questions about the science and psychology of the Life Transformation Program and why it works, and much, much more… Available for purchase on DVD or CD by calling toll-free 877.582.5850 or visiting www.HippocratesInstitute.org.

Did you know the #1 medical spa in the world is located in West Palm Beach, Florida?

HIPPOCRATES HEALTH INSTITUTE offers you a state-of-the-art educational and lifestyle program in a natural and tropical paradise. For more than 50 years, we have helped people restore health and vitality. This is one experience that will truly last a lifetime.

- Delicious Organic Living Foods
- Wheatgrass & Juice Therapies
- Medical & ONDAMED Analysis
- Ozonated Pools, Sauna & Spas
- Electro-magnetic, Cold Laser & Turbosonic Treatments
- Yoga, Meditation & Qi Gong
- Exercise Classes & Gym
- Skilled Body Work Professionals
- Psychological Counseling and Mind Mastery
  Individual & Group
- Aqua-Chi Detoxification
- Infrared, Oxygen & Hyperbaric Therapies
- Nutritional I.V. Therapy
- Medical & Nutritional Counseling
- Health Shop
- Organic Salon

HIPP CRATES
HEALTH INSTITUTE
THE MIND BODY SPIRIT EXPERIENCE OF A LIFETIME

For a free brochure and DVD,
visit our website www.HippocratesInstitute.org
or call us toll free at 1-800-842-2125

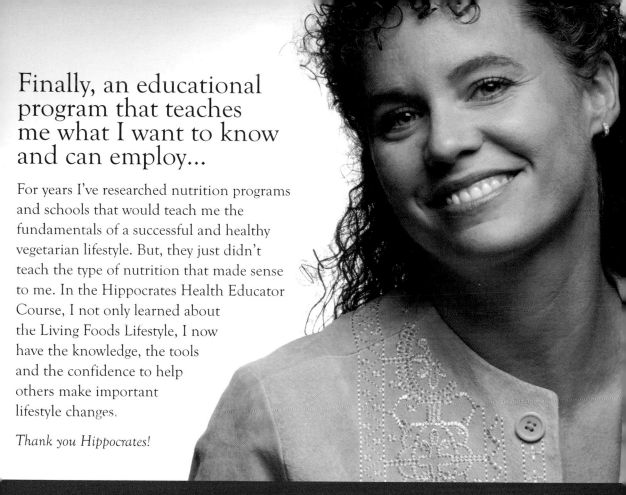

Finally, an educational program that teaches me what I want to know and can employ...

For years I've researched nutrition programs and schools that would teach me the fundamentals of a successful and healthy vegetarian lifestyle. But, they just didn't teach the type of nutrition that made sense to me. In the Hippocrates Health Educator Course, I not only learned about the Living Foods Lifestyle, I now have the knowledge, the tools and the confidence to help others make important lifestyle changes.

Thank you Hippocrates!

HIPPOCRATES LIFEGIVE PRODUCTS

AdrenaSupport is a traditional, herbal formula that helps to support and balance natural, healthy adrenal function and offers long-term adrenal strengthening.

Aloe Vera Fresh is a living food Fresh-Frozen Aloe Vera Gel/Juice cultivated from the Barbadensis-Miller-Stockton species that is grown in organic coral rock containing no preservatives, chemicals, or added water. Aloe Vera Fresh brings your body the most comprehensive way to hydrate itself. Furthermore, it increases nutritional absorption, not only from the aloe, but also all other nutrients that are consumed in both food and whole-food supplement form.

Aphanin is a soil-based dietary supplement recommended for everyone. Vitamin B-12 is an essential vitamin, especially for those with low RBC (red blood cell) count. B-12 increases hemoglobin (iron) levels in the blood and provides energy. LifeGive™ B-12 Forte may also be helpful with Gastro-Intestinal disorders.

B-12 Forte is a soil-based dietary supplement recommended for everyone. Vitamin B-12 is an essential vitamin, especially for those with low RBC (red blood cell) count. B-12 increases hemoglobin (iron) levels in the blood and provides energy. LifeGive™ B-12 Forte may also be helpful with Gastro-Intestinal disorders.

Biotic Guard contains life supporting, healthy bacteria which populate the digestive tract (specifically the small and large intestines) and are integral to the function of digestion, cell development, and the immune system. This superior and powerful probiotic is a soil-based organism formula comprised of a matrix of pure food-derived probiotics and healthy bacteria from organic soil.

Body is freeze-dried Aphanizomenon flos-aquae (AFA) which is the earth's first living food! The blue-green algae is harvested wild from Upper Klamath Lake in Oregon. A special proprietary process assures you the highest standard of purity.

Vitamin C is the premier source for enzymatically rich Vitamin C and bioflavonoids. Unlike Vitamin C supplements that contain isolated synthetic ascorbic acid, LifeGive™ Vitamin C is 100% pure whole food, which may be fully utilized by the body. The Synergy Company, the leading formulator and manufacturer of living food, created this incomparable source of Vitamin C especially for the Hippocrates Health Institute. LifeGive™ Vitamin C is made of wildcrafted camu camu and amla berries, together with a potpourri of organically grown sprouts, berries and other fruits.

CardioKick is a natural supplement that is specifically formulated to support cardiovascular health, naturally assisting blood fluidity and reducing platelet aggregation.

Chemozin is a unique nutrient and herbal supplement that supports the cellular system during and after the use of chemotherapy. This is achieved without interfering with the desired effect of nuclear medicine, yet it helps to preserve the multitude of healthy cells while potentiating some forms of chemotherapy, making them more effective in their process of destroying mutagenic cells.

Chlorella is a single cell Green Algae. It is an excellent source of protein that is easily digested. Chlorella has many benefits to assist in the achievement of optimal wellbeing. It helps the body to get more out of vitamins and minerals. It is helpful with blood sugar regulation, for both Hyper and Hypo glycemic episodes. Chlorella detoxifies the body of heavy metals. Additionally, it may be helpful before and after Chemotherapy or any procedure involving radiation or x-rays.

Enterorinse acts as an overall cellular system repairman, often utilized in the conquest to overcome cancer. This unique nutrient and herbal complex induces cell differentiation, normalizes cell signals, helps to inhibit cancer cell proliferation, induces apoptosis in cancer cells, inhibits angiogenesis, and up-regulates natural immune response.

Est-Toll is a whole-food supplement containing naturally occurring Indole 3-acetic acid, Enzymes, and other vital life-giving nutrients from raw organic cabbage. Studies indicate that the Indole compound is especially helpful for balancing hormones, regulating sleep, as well as strengthening the immune system. Most Indole products on the market are synthetically based, even if they are sold as 'natural'. LifeGive™ Est-Toll stands apart as purely whole food and plant based and is a Naturally Occurring Standard certified product.

Exhilarate is an aloe, amino acid and herbal formula borne out of decades of research and clinical application concerning the positive effects GABA protein has on those suffering with depression. Research reveals that amino acids play a critical role in the function and maintenance of a healthy brain. When these vital nutrients can be replenished to restore proper levels, there is great potential for mental well-being.

HHI-Zyme is Hippocrates Health Institute's own improved time-tested formula that provides essential nutrients, vitamins, minerals and enzymes to enhance digestion of food, increases the electromagnetic frequency around the cell, and helps fight off free radical damage, which is the cause of disease and aging.

Hormone Power works to optimize the body's hormone levels and ratios, while also working to create a healthier internal environment.

Internal Cleanser is a symbiotic combination of nutrients and body activators that first builds and then cleanses the colon by reaching the deepest canyons where unwanted matter resides. It's bases is bioactive chlorophyll-rich algae.

KindKidney is a traditional, herbal formula that supports healthy kidney function and offers a nutritional healing approach for long-term kidney health. Healthy kidney function is vital to overall health and wellbeing, as the kidneys are a very important part of our body's toxin elimination systems. Nutrition and ingestion of proper food and nutrients is necessary for good health and just as necessary is the elimination of toxins from our circulatory system as provided by our kidneys.

Liv-A-Lot is an all-natural herbal formula used traditionally for rejuvenation and purification of the liver. It is an effective blood purifier that fine-tunes the liver and assists in its healthy function as a major detoxifying organ. LifeGive™ Liv-A-Lot can be used periodically when well. It may also be used specifically when presented with any liver challenges.

Live Fresh-Frozen Blue-Green Algae is Fresh Frozen Blue-Green Algae (Aphanizomenon flos-aquae), which is the Earth's first living food harvested wild from Upper Klamath Lake in Oregon. A special proprietary process assures you are getting the highest standard of purity. By adding LifeGive™ Live to your diet you will be receiving the most balanced, complete, nutrient-rich food on Earth providing you with the highest protein and trace mineral concentration of any natural food.

Note: these statements have not been evaluated by the Food and Drug Administration. These products are not intended to diagnose, treat, cure or prevent any disease.

MeltAway is a fat-consuming enzyme complex that is a pure safe and proven way to help the body to eliminate unwanted weight. The enzymes, Lipase and Amylase, assist the digestive and eliminative systems in their quest to rid the body of unwanted lipids. LifeGive™ MeltAway is based and formulated on a historic tradition that has been scientifically validated over many years of research.

Men's Formula is a complete 100% natural whole food multiple vitamin, mineral & herbal formula created especially for Hippocrates Health Institute. This extraordinary hydroponically grown formula blends the wisdom of ancient healing traditions with the best of modern science. Rejuvenating synergized botanicals enhance and strengthen men's distinct needs helping to balance hormone levels and control mood swings.

Ocean Energy is a vegetarian friendly B-12 formula containing nutrients from the land and ocean with added pro-biotics. The combination of nutrients work synergistically to enhance energy and endurance, help to increase Hemoglobin (iron) levels in the blood, and is an excellent alternative to Bee Pollen. For best results, a three-month protocol is recommended.

Par-A-Gone is a natural traditional botanical formula that has been used historically for the elimination of parasites from the body. It is bioactive and contains naturally occurring enzymes and oxygen.

Phys-Neur Omega Oil is a vegetarian friendly essential fatty acid matrix that powerfully nourishes the cells throughout the body, especially the brain. This unique one of a kind omega oil source addresses three anatomical functions. First, it provides complete protein with which each of its seed ingredients are endowed. Second, it offers the most comprehensive fatty acid profile for body and brain function. Third, its phytochemistry, provided by cranberry seeds, black raspberry seeds and organic primrose oil assists neuron activity in the brain for greater alertness, mental acuity, and comprehension.

Phyto-Turmeric and **Phyto-Enhanced** are powerful whole food turmeric supplements with active "curcuminoids" that contain a symphony of disease inhibiting elements such as vitamins, minerals, and enzymes. Each capsule is power packed with pure, naturally occurring curcuminoids, which have been scientifically shown to enhance brain function, offer anti-cancer effects, as well as contain pro-digestive and anti-inflammatory properties.

Pinnacle is a comprehensive Thyroid Complex which balances hormones, supports a healthy metabolic rate, and aids in fat metabolism and detoxification. This unique product is complete comprehensive nourishment for healthy Thyroid function. It contains only quantum quality nutrients, exquisitely well-grown and free of any toxic tagalongs.

Power Powder is the purest and most potent green food supplement made with organic ingredients. The Synergy Company, the pioneer in formulating and manufacturing enzymatically rich and organic superfoods, created LifeGive™ Power Powder exclusively for Hippocrates Health Institute. Packed with more than 60 vibrant ingredients, LifeGive™ Power Powder is a superior source of highly beneficial phytonutrients that are helpful for building muscle and gaining strength. In combination with a healthy lifestyle, LifeGive™ Power Powder promotes sustained energy and well-being.

Radiance is an age-defying skin balancing crème that is very easily absorbed. It tones and textures skin, fades dark unsightly spots, minimizes wrinkles, gives a more youthful look to skin, tightens skin to reduce sagging, and prevents skin dehydration. This product fights damaging lipid peroxidation and protects skin mitochondria from dangerous free radicals. LifeGive™ Radiance facilitates the stimulating effects of the epidermal growth factor and is used to correct a variety of skin conditions.

Reverse is a naturally occurring bioactive source of Ubiquinol Coenzyme Q10 made from probiotics used to "reverse" cellular damage caused by aging as the CoQ10 levels in the body naturally decrease. This unique nutrient may support normal heart function, protect cells from free-radical induced oxidative damage, provide anti-aging effects, and help maintain healthy energy levels. CoQ10 exists in both ubiquinol and ubiquinone forms. Ubiquinol works better because it raises blood levels of CoQ10 much more quickly and naturally.

Sun-D offers a superior naturally occurring vegan source of Vitamin D3 with Vitamin D precursors from Shiitake mushrooms and rice germ extracts. This powerful plant source of life-supporting and living Vitamin D may be used for the support of good health, prevention of nutrient deficiencies, and the prevention of the development of threatening health conditions.

Systemic Enzymes is formulated with proteolytic enzymes, Vitamin C, and select botanical antioxidants that have been specifically chosen for their ability to combat oxidative stress, support healthy circulation, support muscle and joint recovery after exercise, and provide other systemic benefits.

Veg-Cal is a whole food plant based for of Calcium which provides the best source of this corner stone mineral. Fortification will ward off deficiencies that can lead to osteoporosis, osteopenia, rheumatism, and intestinal cancers. It can be consumed daily, each capsule containing 15mg of plant based bio-available whole food calcium taken from Terminalia Arjuna (a land plant) which manifests a unique trace mineral profile including magnesium, zinc, manganese, along with other important elements. Additionally, Terminalia Arjuna is traditionally used to enhance and protect cardiovascular health.

Women's Formula is a complete, 100% natural, whole food multiple vitamin, mineral, and herbal formula, created especially for Hippocrates Health Institute. This extraordinary, hydroponically grown formula blends the wisdom of ancient healing traditions with the best of modern science. Exquisite flower essences and synergized botanicals are included to nurture women's special needs and natural rhythms, helping to balance hormone levels and control mood swings. Offers women of all ages (12 and older) unprecedented levels of nutritional support and energy.

For more information about LifeGive products and other Hippocrates offerings, call Hippocrates Mail Order today 1-877-582-5850 or visit www.HippocratesInstitute.org

LIVING FOODS FOR OPTIMUM HEALTH
By Brian R. Clement, PhD, NMD, LN

An introduction to the Hippocrates' Living Foods Lifestyle that for over 50 years has helped hundreds of thousands of people overcome chronic diseases such as cancer, diabetes, heart disease, chronic fatigue syndrome, fibromyalsia, arthritis, candidiasis, depression, and more to lead fulfilling and happy lives. Written by one of the world's foremost authorities on Living Foods, Hippocrates Health Institute's Co-Director Dr. Brian Clement.

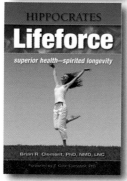

HEALTH & HEALING:
A Families' Guide to Home Remedies from the Heart
By Anna Maria Clement, PhD, NMD, LN

A beautifully illustrated 120-page guide of practical, time-tested home remedies offering suggestions on using herbs, essential oils and other natural therapies for addressing a wide variety of illnesses and creating a healthy home environment. This comprehensive book from a mother of four and Hippocrates' Co-Director Dr. Anna Maria Clement is a must for every home library.

SUPPLEMENTS EXPOSED:
The truth they don't want you to know about vitamins, minerals, and their effects on your health
By Brian R. Clement, PhD, NMD, LN

Nutrition expert Dr. Brian Clement explores the various myths that have made supplements a "buyer beware" industry. *Supplements Exposed* strips away layers of deception to reveal the truth about what millions of supplement users each year have taken for granted.

LIFEFORCE
Superior Health—Spirited Longevity
By Brian R. Clement, PhD, NMD, LN

Lifeforce is a compilation of Dr. Clement's four decades of first-hand experience with the living foods program and from Hippocrates Health Institute's 50-year history with hundreds of thousands of people from around the globe. Practical, straightforward and user friendly, this book will positively guide you into a happy and healthy life.

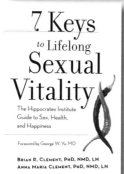

7 KEYS TO LIFELONG SEXUAL VITALITY:
The Hippocrates Health Institute Guide to Sex, Health, and Happiness
By Brian R. Clement, PhD, NMD, LN
and Anna Maria Clement, PhD, NMD, LN

Health and sex experts Drs. Brian and Anna Maria Clement view sexual energy as a universal fuel of life that nourishes mind, body, and spirit. They believe that remaining sexually active is one of the most effective ways to naturally enhance your health and your life. 7 Keys to Lifelong Sexual Vitality offers health nutrition, detoxification, and exercise tips for all ages. These suggestions are all natural and require no drugs.

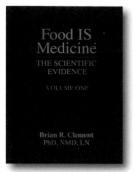

FOOD IS MEDICINE:
The Scientific Evidence, Volume One
By Brian R. Clement, PhD, NMD, LN

This is the first of a three-volume series by Dr. Brian Clement, contributed to public education. *Food IS Medicine* offers the nutritional science of how disease prevention and increased longevity can be achieved by proper food choices. The most important ingested medicine comes from the very food we consume, and now the most noteworthy and provocative studies that clearly demonstrate this fact are available in one place.

KILLER CLOTHES:
How Seemingly Innocent Clothing Choices Endanger Your Health…
and How to Protect Yourself!
*By Brian R. Clement, PhD, NMD, LN
and Anna Maria Clement, PhD, NMD, LN*

Discover the toxic truth about the garments we wear and the harmful health effects of clothing once considered safe. Learn what fabrics and chemicals to watch for when selecting clothing, why to avoid any garment that has anti-odor, antistatic, antimicrobial, etc., tips for ecological and health-friendly cleaning, and the advantages of natural fabrics.

KILLER FISH:
How Eating Aquatic Life Endangers Your Health
By Brian R. Clement, PhD, NMD, LN

Despite many mainstream nutrition experts claiming fish is a healthful alternative to red meat and dairy products, alarming numbers of scientific reports and government agencies dispute this common assumption. In *Killer Fish*, Dr. Brian Clement shines a compelling light on the perils of marine life and the waterways we share, and offers invaluable suggestions for nutritious dietary alternatives to aquatic fare.

LONGEVITY:
Enjoying Long Life Without Limits
By Brian R. Clement, PhD, NMD, LN

Dr. Brian Clement and his team at Hippocrates Health Institute have developed a state of the art program for health and recovery. The hundreds of thousands of participants in the program over the last half-century give Clement a privileged insight into the lifestyle required to maintain youth, vitality and stamina. *Longevity* delivers this cutting edge knowledge, coupled with a common sense practical approach that will raise your level of health and happiness.

Subscribe FREE Today!
Join thousands who have achieved greater health through the Hippocrates Life Transformation Program. Call toll free 1.800.842.2125 or 561.471.8876 and order your *FREE subscription* to the Hippocrates Health Institute Magazine: *Healing Our World.*

HIPP CRATES
HEALTH INSTITUTE

1443 Palmdale Court
West Palm Beach, Florida 33411
www.HippocratesInstitute.org